trying

Love, Loss and Stop Asking if I'm Pregnant Yet

BARBARA NUDDLE

This work depicts actual events in the life of the author as truthfully as recollection permits. While all persons within are actual individuals, names and identifying characteristics have been changed in some instances to respect their privacy.

Life Out Loud Productions
Montclair, NJ

Copyright ©2022 Barbara Nuddle

Cover:
   Anish Kapoor
   When I am Pregnant, 1992
   Fiberglass and paint
   Dimensions variable
   Collection: Nasjonalmuseet, Oslo, Norway
   ©Anish Kapoor, 2018
   Photo by Andreas Harvik

More information at www.trying-thebook.com

ISBN: 978-0-692-11093-5
LCCN: 2022919997

All rights reserved, which includes the right to reproduce this book or portions thereof in any form whatsoever except as provided by the U.S. Copyright Law. For information address Life Out Loud Productions.

Publisher's Cataloging-in-Publication (Provided by Cassidy Cataloguing Services, Inc.)
Names: Nuddle, Barbara, author.
Title: Trying : love, loss and stop asking if I'm pregnant yet / Barbara Nuddle.
Description: Montclair, NJ : Life Out Loud, [2022]
Identifiers: ISBN: 9780692110935 | LCCN: 2022919997
Subjects: LCSH: Infertility, Female--Psychological aspects. | Women--Biography. | Childlessness--Psychological aspects. | Motherhood--Psychological aspects. | Mothers and daughters. | Man-woman relationships. | Parents--Death--Psychological aspects. | Interfaith marriage. | Loss (Psychology) | LCGFT: Autobiographies.
Classification: LCC: RG201 .N84 2022 | DDC: 618.178--dc23

To Sydney

The First Chapter

I'm tired of waking up every morning and feeling my breasts. While still lying in bed, I check them for any change in size or tenderness. Then I walk over to the bathroom mirror where I examine my nipples for any changes in color or shape. It's way too early for me to be that involved with my body. I like to have coffee first.

"If you were pregnant, you'd know it," my friend, Jeptha, told me over lunch the other day. I was desperately in need of a glass of wine but afraid I'd inebriate anyone who might be forming in my body. As our waitress stood by our table awaiting our drink order, I quickly slid my hand underneath my sweater to re-check my breasts.

"I knew *immediately*," Jeptha assured me, watching my sweater come alive. Our waitress rocked nervously side to side. She's 22. What does *she* know about wanting to be pregnant? She's probably got five condoms in her purse and is on the pill. Again, Jeptha tried to reassure me. "I had a glass of wine when I was pregnant and didn't realize it, and it was fine."

"You just told me you *absolutely* knew," I said.

"Oh. That was another time."

"I'll have the wine," I told the waitress, who took our order and then ran toward the exit pulling a cigarette from her pocket.

The woman who gives me facials didn't know. One month, she had intense cramping on her left side, took Dong Quai (a Chinese herb thought to bring on your period), then found out she was pregnant after all. "I was so surprised!" she told me, while examining my pores under her huge magnifying lens. "We weren't even trying."

Surprise would be nice. I'd love for pregnancy to sneak up on me like a tiny pimple that gets bigger and bigger by the day. That way, I wouldn't have to think about what it means to try.

When my husband, Oliver and I first started trying, I worried that the trouble I was having conceiving wasn't that I *couldn't* have a baby, but that I *wouldn't* have a baby—not without my mother. She had died years before, along with my father, in a hotel fire. And the thought of having a child without my mother ever seeing him—or her—horrified me.

The year of their sudden death, my gynecologist told me, "Get married. Have a baby. Make a family of your own."

Was he nuts? I was just beginning to deal with the fact that my parents would never meet the man I would marry. The last thing I wanted to do was have a baby.

When I was nine years old, I heard the word "fuck" for the first time while standing in the Lost and Found with my friend, Debbie Albert, looking for my red mitten. Debbie told me it was something men do to women. "It's not a bad thing," she said. "But it's how babies are born." That afternoon, while my mother and I were driving to Strawbridge and Clothier in search of an 80-inch, oblong tablecloth for our dining room table, I told her that I knew about the "f-word."

"Well," she said, her voice rising to an embarrassing volume she always excused as her "teacher voice." "When you are *married*, a man places his penis inside your vagina, plants his seed, and that is how babies are born. Daddy and I call that making love," she said, rolling up the car window. "But some people call that 'fuck,'" and she got out of the car.

That night, when she came into my room to say

goodnight, she sat on my bed and said, "Now I want you to feel free to ask me anything you want to about sex." So I asked her, "I understand about the making the baby part. It's the other part I don't understand—the making love part. How will I know where to put my hands?"

"You'll just know," she said, and walked out of the room.

Maybe if my mother was still alive, she'd have more to say about the making love part. No, she wouldn't. She'd say nothing. But nothing is something. And in my fantasy, I would get pregnant and things would feel normal. I haven't felt normal for a long time.

When I was in my early twenties, I moved to New York, worked on Seventh Avenue, and prided myself on being too busy to date. That didn't stop me from collecting outfits I'd wear on dates with men I had yet to meet. I used to reassure my concerned Jewish mother that I would get married someday. I'd use my favorite line from the movie, *Gigi*, "Women like us don't get married at once. We get married . . . at last." When they told me my parents had died, I was 26 years old. I suddenly felt like I'd waited too long.

It's been 10 years. I just left a consultation with a team of infertility specialists. It seems that while I was desperately trying to become someone other than a daughter, a wife or a mother, I may have, once again, waited too long.

Trying

Honeymoon Misconceptions

Oliver and I agreed to begin trying to make a baby on our honeymoon, which we took three months after our wedding. The night before we left, I stared at my stack of T-shirts, underwear, and little white "sleep" socks and realized I should probably pack the sexy little negligee my friend Mary gave me at my bridal shower. I remember that when I held up this lacy, low-cut number, everyone applauded, and then laughed. They knew me. It was never coming out of the box. Oliver says I go to bed with more clothing than most people wear on the street.

Now, as I pulled my wardrobe together, I was feeling the pressures of honeymoon sex. This wasn't just a vacation. This was the trip that celebrates our union. We were supposed to take each other to levels of ecstasy I'd only read about in my nail salon. And this wouldn't just be sex—we'd be trying to make a baby! Suddenly, I wasn't so sure I was ready to become somebody's mother.

"Oliver," I said, walking into our second bedroom where he was pulling out suitcases from the closet. "I think we should consider dating other people." I stared at my husband—this man I might have a child with—and couldn't believe I married someone with blond hair. I never went for guys with blond hair. My mother had blond hair. Oh my God, I married my mother!

When I first met Oliver, he asked me what my mother

looked like. "She looked like Angela Lansbury. What did *your* mother look like?"

"You're not going to believe me," he said, astonished. "But *she* looked like Angela Lansbury!"

Oliver told me stories of how his mother used to love walking along the beach in California, gathering stones and lugging them home in the bottom of her skirt. Or how, at the dinner table, to save calories, she'd eat only the middle out of a Rich's chocolate éclair. I learned to love Oliver's mother through his stories, and I saw Oliver as the kind of guy who could love my mother through mine.

Early in our relationship, Oliver and I felt comfortable—solid. We became each other's family. But the night before our honeymoon, I told him I wasn't ready to start one of our own.

"Re–lax," he said. "We'll see how it goes." But the minute we entered our junior suite on the Amalfi coast, the one with a balcony draped in bougainvillea overlooking the sea, Oliver announced, "What a great place to start a family!"

Our first moonlit night, as we made love to the sounds of the waves crashing against the cliff, I looked into Oliver's eyes and said, "Promise me if I get pregnant we can turn the dining room into my office." I wanted to be sure I'd still have a room of my own.

As it turned out, the honeymoon was no big opportunity for conceiving since I soon realized I had no idea when I was ovulating. I had used the counting method (the length of an average cycle minus 14 days) to determine the time in my cycle when an egg would be ready to be released and hopefully fertilized. My period came early so I guess I counted wrong. Oliver couldn't believe it. "How can you *not* know when you get your period?" he asked, frustrated by our first wasted cycle.

"It's been 20 years," I said. "I stopped paying attention." Besides, I never was one of those women who got overly involved with her cycle. I was the kind of girl who put her hand down her underwear, felt the first strands of puberty, and didn't look again until I saw hair creeping out from my bikini. My mother, the teacher, left a series of pamphlets on my bed that she'd gotten from the nurse at her school entitled, *Growing Up and Loving It*. And I once watched a movie at school—the one that only the girls went to—that told us, "You, too, can go bowling during your period." And that pretty much covered it. I knew even less about ovulation. I was 36 years old when I finally understood that there are only three days in a month that you can even *get* pregnant.

My gynecologist was the gynecologist to the stars. He had a bustling Park Avenue practice made up of women who worshipped him for helping them get pregnant against all odds, or socialites who adored him for his boyish good looks and charming accent.

Dr. Celebrity used to date my old boss, Phyllis. It would not be unusual for her, after a late night working together with me on Seventh Avenue followed by an even later supper in Chinatown, that she would order twice as much food so we could bring leftovers to the office of Dr. C. We'd arrive at 11 o'clock at night and the office would still be filled with women waiting to see him.

"Do you girls need anything?" he'd ask, looking in our direction before he disappeared into another door.

"Do you need an exam?" my boss asked me, like she was offering me a soda. Even though I hadn't found a gynecologist since moving to New York, I liked my pelvic exams *before* eating a huge meal and *after* slipping into a clean pair of underwear.

I think a weekend bladder infection provided the incentive for me to call Phyllis and have her arrange my first visit with Dr. Celebrity, who, unbelievably on a Sunday night, examined me and dispensed enough drug samples so I could make it home in a taxi without peeing. O.K. Membership has its privileges. From then on, whenever I'd arrive at his standing-room-only office, the receptionist would give me a big smile, send along her regards to my boss, and promise to get me in to see HIM as soon as possible. I'd wait two hours instead of three.

"He's a miracle worker," the women would tell me, patting their bulging stomachs.

For years, I'd sit hour after hour in his office wondering why I put myself through this torture for what was ultimately a thirty-second exam.

Trying

Back then, I didn't need a miracle worker—just a Pap smear. Yet, I stayed on, sensing, fearing that someday, I might.

When I eventually was seen by Dr. C, he'd be in and out of the exam room in the time it took him to say, "You look great! How's your love life? When are you going to make babies?" He ended the exam with a kiss on my cheek before racing off to his next patient.

Finally, when Oliver and I got engaged, I decided to find a doctor who wasn't seen regularly by thousands on the television talk show circuit, holding up his speculum demonstrating his expertise. I wanted someone who was a little less famous and a little more attentive—more hand-holding—for when I was ready to get pregnant. My new gynecologist had delivered three of my girl-friend's babies, and was a woman. I assumed she'd be more empathetic.

On my first visit, I told her I was getting married in six months and planned on trying to get pregnant soon after. I was 35 and asked her if there was anything I should be doing to prepare. She told me I had a nice, long body—good for carrying a pregnancy—and taught me how to track my ovulation by counting. Nothing more was said. We decided I was going to relax and let it happen. I viewed the process in the same way I make my art—by paying attention, but not so much attention that you get in the way of creation.

The Mother Load

Soon after our honeymoon, I was getting into the Jacuzzi at my gym—an activity I didn't know I should avoid if I was serious about trying. I saw this woman, her eyes closed, her body leaning into the jets, getting totally relaxed. When she opened her eyes, she saw me trying to make myself comfortable. I smiled, which she took as an invitation to converse.

"I'm having my kid's birthday party this afternoon—30 kids and 30 adults," she said. "I'm a wreck! Got any kids?"

"No," I said. "I just got married. Well, actually I got married in June."

"You got married in June? June is the greatest month. That's when my second was born. And you know what? I had them both underwater. Absolutely no pain when you have them underwater."

I was speechless.

"In here," she said, pointing into the water, "you're constantly lubricated. You know, it's not the contractions themselves that are so painful. It's having dry skin that makes it unbearable. All that in and out, in and out, in and out."

Her face strongly resembled a blowfish while she spoke. "After the birth, the baby just swims around outside of you—still attached! No need to cut the cord yet. For God's sake, they're in water for nine months!"

I suddenly felt uncomfortable sharing warm, bubbly water with this woman and I got out. She kept going. "Water-birthing is like having a midwife massage the inside of your, you know . . ." she said, making this motion with her two fingers going round and round in a circle. O.K. I'm done. Bye.

But before I left, I leaned over and said, "You know, my husband and I are starting to try. And to tell you the truth," I continued, thinking that, in some magical way, this woman with a unicorn tattooed on her shoulder could advise me, "I don't think I can get pregnant because I'm afraid to have a baby without my own . . ." I stopped. I decided I didn't want to share my theory with this woman—the one about not getting pregnant because I still longed for my own mother. Instead, I gave her my other line—the one that sounded funnier, more appropriate for gym conversation and locker room chats. "I'm afraid to give up my office!" I said, then laughed, trying to convince her—and me—that it was as simple as that. I walked toward the showers.

"Visualize!" she yelled back. "Feel that there is room for a baby and there will be!"

I walked home that day trying to find a space in my body for mothers and daughters and my child-to-be.

The Science of Ovulation

The next morning, I decided I was ready to try what several

new mothers had been telling me to do all along—get an ovulation kit. The test I bought involved so many test tubes you needed a lab coat to perform them. I couldn't leave the house for an hour. The process was a little like doing laundry for heavily soiled items when you have to run back into the room every five minutes to throw another ingredient into the rinse cycle.

Performing all these rituals made me feel better—like I was finally ready to have a child. My whole life I've felt like I'm *not* exactly ready. Maybe it's because I was born two weeks early.

"The doctor said you were ready to come out," my mother loved telling me. "So I went to the hospital, they put me to sleep, and when I woke up, there you were—my little princess."

Her doctor thought I was ready, but was *I*?

When I was 12 years old, my Grandmom Belle died. I remember going with my mother to my grandmother's house to pack up all of her clothes. I sat on the wooden staircase leading up to my grandmother's bedroom, listening to the sound of my mother rummaging through the closet, then to the sound of clothes along with their hangers being shoved into a bag. When my mother appeared at the top of the stairs, I said to her, "Mommy, I feel so badly that you don't have your mommy anymore."

She sat down next to me and said, "Barbie, I don't need my mommy the way *you* need me. And when I die, you won't need a mommy the way you need me right now."

Trying

She was wrong. Ten years after her death, I still see myself, above all else, as a daughter. Embarking on a family of my own, I feel the pangs of forced separation all over again.

"Do you feel nauseous?" Oliver asked me, after our first few months of trying, looking for the first sign of pregnancy.

"I'm nauseous *every* morning," I told him.

When I was little, I'd wake up with a sick feeling in my stomach after spending the whole night worrying about dying. I was consumed with wondering what happens after I die? The blackness will be endless. Me not being here—unaware of life—forever and ever. It made me nauseous.

I asked my mother, "Where was I when George Washington crossed the Delaware? Is that the same place I'll be when I'm dead?"

I was afraid to go to school. Often, when I got there, I'd get that queasy feeling in my stomach that wouldn't go away until the teacher called my mother and had her talk to me. The feeling was especially bad if it was raining and we had indoor recess in the lunchroom with the smell of shepherd's pie filtering through the air.

These days, the minute I wake up I hear the voice, "It's a new day! You've done nothing since graduate school! Do something amazing! Make a film. Write a screenplay! Get a *real* job!" Already, I'm nauseous.

Caffeine is usually the remedy for my anxiety. But

since we've been trying, caffeine is forbidden. Instead, I've been drinking red clover tea to balance my female energies. I can't tell if it's the semi-sweet tea or my nerves that are making me sick, but at least I'm trying. However, there are days when receiving a jolt from caffeine feels more important to me than conception and I down a cup or two.

The days I go into my kitchen and succumb to a good cup of coffee are the days I hate myself for not wanting a baby enough. What kind of a mother wouldn't give up coffee? My mother had this way of drinking from the same mug of coffee all day long, no matter what its temperature. We'd sit at the kitchen table for hours on Saturdays talking about my friends and hers. On the subject of my boyfriends, she'd say, "Are you asking me what I think as your mother or as your friend?" I never saw the difference.

After using the ovulation kit for the first time, I noticed the instructions specifically said to use *tap* water. I used Evian, thinking bottled would surely be better. I was wrong. I always seem to make mistakes. I think I do it on purpose so that I have an alternative explanation for why something doesn't work out. It gives me space. And in that space lives both what I want and the fear of getting it.

After six months of trying, I decided to make a call.

Trying

Help Wanted

Part of me was still scared of motherhood, yet I needed to know if there was something wrong with my body. My gynecologist suggested I go for a test called an HSG (hysterosalpingogram), which involves injecting a dye through your tubes to check for any blockages. I was nervous but excited to have this procedure. Often, they say, the test, itself, can "blow out your tubes," making conception easier.

After the test, I waited a week to hear from my doctor. Nothing. Why wasn't she calling? Did she see something horrible and was waiting for a second opinion? Whatever the reason, the wait was excruciating. Desperate, I had Oliver's internist call for my results. My doctor never called because she was swamped with deliveries and then left on vacation. So much for hand-holding.

Oliver's internist told me I had several fibroid tumors blocking my tubes, but they could be removed through surgery. When someone from my doctor's office finally called, they told me the same. I needed surgery. Fine—but not with her.

There was a voice inside my head. The one that always told me I'd have trouble getting pregnant. The one that told me to stay with Dr. Celebrity in case I needed a miracle. That voice led me back to Park Avenue. As a doctor, he may be a maniac. But as a surgeon, he was one of the best.

The receptionist remembered me and, just like old times, ushered me in as soon as possible. The two hours I spent waiting for my consultation were filled chatting off and on with her about her son's wedding, her in-laws, and the Dior gown she bought for the occasion. "When else will I have an excuse to buy Dior?" she said, before calling in the next patient. I mentioned to her that Oliver and I were planning a trip to Budapest.

"Are you staying at the Gallért? They have the best shower caps." Then she wrote down the names of her favorite four-star restaurants. This really was a full-service organization.

When I finally sat down in Dr. C's office, a room I rarely saw, he got right to the point. In addition to recommending a hysteroscopy—in which the doctor uses a telescope-like device to look at the inside of your uterus and remove any abnormal tissue growth—he also recommended I undergo a laparoscopy. This procedure involves examining your reproductive organs through a tiny scope inserted through the belly button. He scheduled both procedures five days later.

I'd never had surgery before. Not a stitch. So, the idea of someone knocking me out and sticking their hands up my vagina was not exactly thrilling me. I already had intimacy issues. This could put me back in therapy. I spoke to several people who used Dr. Celebrity for surgery. They told me I could trust him and I did.

Trying

After the surgery, I remember waking up from the anesthesia and hearing him say something about my right side being blocked, but that I would be "able to make babies." Oliver saw him racing through the waiting room and cornered him to find out how it went. "You should have no problem making plenty of babies," he said, then quickly shook Oliver's hand, and left.

That was it. No further instructions? What saved my sanity was a promise from the nurse, who assured me the doctor would answer all my questions at my follow-up appointment. That day came and he saw me for the usual 30 seconds. "You're fine," he said, taking a fast look at my stitches.

"Really? I wasn't sure if I should be . . ." I said to his back as he was already turning to leave the room. Hey! This was supposed to be my moment. I was desperate for more information. He was desperate to move on to his next patient.

"You want Clomid? I'll give you Clomid," he said, opening the exam room door. "Take it on day five of your period, then . . ." I stopped listening. I got up, got dressed, put on my sunglasses to hide my streaming tears, passed the receptionist and said, "I can't do this anymore."

I walked up Madison Avenue sobbing looking like Mary Tyler Moore after a bad day in the newsroom. My eyes followed the well-dressed shoppers entering the

Armani store or walking past me with a bag from Valentino. I got a few stares from the beautiful people dining at the sidewalk cafes. What? The women of Prozac nation never had a bad day?

I felt so wounded by his brush-off, I didn't want to speak—even to a cab driver. I got on the crosstown bus where my yoga instructor was seated by the door. She yelled out my name, happy to see me, then noticed I'd been crying.

"Let's just say," I said, as I took a seat next to her, "I'm looking forward to returning to your class so I can be nice to my body again and leave it at that."

When you're trying, everything takes weeks and weeks. Tests can only be performed at certain points in your cycle, and one month turns into two before you get to take the next step. That's why women are infertile for years. You can only DO something about it three or four days a month. So, Oliver and I took the vacation we'd planned before my surgery. We toured Prague, Budapest and then Salzburg, which is where they filmed the movie *The Sound of Music*. One day, we climbed up and down the steps in the gardens where Julie Andrews sings "Doe, a deer." As I watched Oliver round up other peoples' children to accompany me singing the additional verses, just like in the movie, I knew I was ready to have his children. And the receptionist was right—the Gellért Hotel *did* have excellent shower caps.

Trying

When we got home, I went to yet another gynecologist. He was the first doctor to give me an FSH test. This is a blood test typically performed on the third day of your menstrual cycle (aka "day 3") that measures my body's ability to produce follicle-stimulating hormone—the main hormone involved in producing eggs. He called the next day and immediately referred me to an infertility specialist.

At the Office of Reproductive Medicine

Walking into the office was my first dose of reality. This wasn't an office that displayed pamphlets featuring glossy color photographs of a mother nuzzling her baby in a field of flowers, or offered advice on breast-feeding, parenting, or mother-care products. These booklets featured black and white photographs of couples holding hands, walking on the beach, or just titles: *Infertility over 35*, *Infertility: the Emotional Roller Coaster*, and *Insights into Infertility*.

Infertility. The word makes me feel like I'm already infertile. I wasn't infertile. My husband, Oliver and I were still trying. But it seemed I leapt from "trying" to "infertile" just by walking through the door. In that office, every woman, every couple, was there because they could not conceive normally. Leaflets on hormone replacements, advertisements for drug stores that specialize in carrying them, and fliers from local support groups were provided for the patients. I touched nothing. These *other* people were infertile. I was there to *see* if I was infertile.

Oliver grabbed a newspaper, sat down and read. I scoped out the other women. The one with the good shoe, black pantsuit, and designer handbag probably lived nearby on the East Side. Another woman, wearing an orange short outfit and sandals, was obviously not from the Metropolitan area, which meant she must have traveled some distance to come here. These doctors must *really* be good.

When I was a little girl, my mother used to take me on the train into downtown Philadelphia to see the Christmas tree at Wanamaker's Department store. As I sat looking out the window, my head pressed against the glass watching the tracks merge into one another, my mother read the paper. We looked up as several people entered our car.

"Ehem . . . shoes," my mother said, her head hidden behind her paper.

"What?" I asked, scanning her newspaper for some sort of advertisement.

"Shoo–ooes!" she repeated, raising her head above the newspaper and rotating her eyes toward the seat across from us.

I looked over and saw a woman wearing red chunky-heeled shoes with candy canes strapped onto the laces. I smiled. Once we arrived downtown, my mother briskly parted the crowds on Walnut Street and navigated our path by squeezing my hand, then calling out, "Hat!" "Coat!" "Shoe!" "Pocketbook!" Any item of clothing that she decided shouldn't make an appearance that season, she felt the need to comment on. It wasn't that *we* were so well-dressed. It was just our way of observing the world.

The woman sitting across from me in the business suit looked older, maybe 45. She must feel fortunate to have fertility options at her age. That's not me. I'm 36, wearing black jeans and a white T-shirt. I wanted to look casual but appropriate, sophisticated but not old, slim but not anorexic. I wanted to look fertile—too young and healthy for any of this to be happening.

Eventually, husbands joined the women. Each of them kissed their wives hello and complained about the traffic or the heat. I had to believe they were thinking, "Can you believe we're here because we need serious help making a baby?"

One guy looked like a Wall Street type. Nice suit. Black slicked-back hair. Handsome. Very handsome. I wondered what it was like for him and his wife to have scheduled sex. Did he come racing home from work midday, eagerly ripping off his suit and tie? Or was he tense and exhausted from "performing," then having to help his wife hold her legs up in the air? Trying isn't just sex. It's the pelvis-tilting, sperm settling, follow-through that's critical. I imagined this attractive couple having sex before infertility. Then I imagined Mr. Wall Street having sex with me on the floor of his living room. I hated myself for that.

The waiting room was large with a seating area divided into two sections. After a little while, one of the nurses came in and announced, "I'm Alice and I need to ask everyone here for class to please scoot over to this side of the room." *Scoot?* I already didn't like this woman. Alice had this way of projecting her voice louder than was necessary for the tiny office, and much louder than I was comfortable with for the subject matter: hormone replacement therapy. Oliver and I were the only couple that did not move over.

Not wanting to make the other couples self-conscious, I hid behind *New York Magazine*'s "Summer Fun" issue while listening to the distinctions between the drugs Pergonal and Fertinex. When I heard Alice rip open a package of what she called, "subcutaneous syringes," I looked up. I watched four couples fondling needles and examining tiny glass bottles. Were their minds really on how to draw the medicine into a needle, or were they wondering, "Why us?"

"Now each of you will have a different required dosage," she warned. "But whether it's one packet or two, it is *very* important to mix the water with each of the dry packets before collecting it in your syringe."

I looked over to Oliver. "Do you use twice as much

water for two packets, or can the same amount be enough to dissolve both packets of dry?"

"You're actually *listening* to this?" he asked, refolding his newspaper, glancing at the next article.

"Aren't *you*?" I said. I couldn't believe that my husband, Mr. "Medical Journalist," Mr. "Vice President of Consumer News for Reuters Health," Mr. "Let's Look Up Your Condition in Five Clinical Research Books from *The New England Journal of Medicine*," was perusing the New York Times "Arts and Leisure" section and missing a live demonstration.

When Oliver and I were first dating, we went to California to spend Christmas with his father. This was a bold move for a Jewish girl. But, on this trip, I discovered two things. One: if we would ever marry, we needed to have a serious Christmas tree discussion. And two: Oliver is excellent in a crisis. During that week, as we were unloading the tree ornaments from the boxes his father kept in the garage, Oliver noticed that his father's breathing was very labored and he was popping extra nitroglycerin tablets. We took his dad to the hospital for a series of tests and learned that he needed a bypass operation. I carefully observed Oliver as he made sure his father felt comfortable, conversed with the doctors, or chased them down the hallway if his questions weren't answered. He acted the way I tried to act when my father had *his* surgeries—fearful, but chatty; exhausted, but relentless; in shock, but highly efficient.

It was one of the reasons I knew I could spend the rest of my life with Oliver. He knows how to deal. He's a good son. I had been a good daughter.

This time, after being married for less than a year, it was my body that wasn't cooperating. I *had* to watch Nurse Alice's demonstration on how to inject hormones into your leg. If this was going to be me some day, I might be too freaked-out sitting in a class with total strangers to remember anything about squeezing my thigh at its fleshiest part to avoid hitting a vein.

The Consultation

The desktop of the doctor's office was stacked with visual aids to which he constantly referred during our consultation. They looked like children's books—the short, chunky ones with lots of color illustrations. Only *these* pages were filled with all the possible scenarios for infertility. My problems, apparently, were on pages three, five, and eight, and he was only on the first book.

"Now, Barbara," the doctor said, "your FSH level is higher than we'd like it to be, and I see here that your mother took D-E-S. Barbara, this may or may not be a concern. And I see, Barbara, that your right side is blocked."

He kept glancing down at the chart to catch my name, and then used it in a sentence as he looked past me toward my husband. "What we might have to do,

Barbara, is give you another round of blood tests to see where your levels fall next month."

Repeating my name did not bring me the comfort he intended. Instead, it revealed the fact that, somewhere along the line, he must have taken a class in patient relations where they tell you to be sure to mention the name of the woman whose ovaries you are examining as many times as possible.

"After the tests, Barbara, we can discuss your options." Options? Which page in your Little Big Books has the word "euphemism" on it? He's telling me they need more information to see if IVF is "the way to go." IVF—or "in vitro fertilization"—is a procedure that involves taking my eggs out of my body, mixing them with my husband's sperm in a dish, and, after a few days of gestation, reinserting the embryos into my body. It's a procedure I vaguely remember hearing about when researchers made the first test-tube baby, but I never gave little Mary What's-Her-Name much thought. I never imagined *I'd* be benefiting from that technological breakthrough. Suddenly, instead of being worried that I'd have to go through IVF, I'm left hoping the procedure is even an option!

Apparently, my FSH levels needed to be below 10 for these doctors to accept me into their program. Mine was 9.5. But my number didn't necessarily indicate my ability to conceive. It just indicated whether I was a good enough candidate for their program. In discussing my potential to conceive, the doctor kept using the word "likelihood" interchangeably with the word "eligibility." I realized we had two different goals in mind.

Why hadn't any of my gynecologists tested my FSH before? Sure, I told them I was willing to "try and see what happens." But when you're 35 years old and your probability of getting pregnant drops to 25 percent, I can't believe this test isn't the *first* thing they do. Shouldn't this test be required for women over 35? In fact, why not take the test whether or not you're thinking about babies, just so you know where you stand?

My consultation with Dr. Repeats-Your-Name-Too-Many-Times concluded with a pelvic exam. This would be my third in the last five weeks. All during my exam, I was subjected to his expressions of disbelief that my mother took the drug DES in 1960. Doctors commonly prescribed DES (diethylstilbestrol) if a woman had a history of miscarriage, diabetes, high blood pressure or slight bleeding during pregnancy. DES was thought to thicken the uterine lining to prevent a miscarriage, but was later found to be a possible cause of cervical cancer, among other things.

"When were you born?" he asked, as I opened my legs, placing my feet in the stirrups. I focused on the little pink cozies covering the stirrups featuring the name of a popular fertility drug.

"1960?" he repeated. "And you were born in Philadelphia?" For a second, I thought about life in Philadelphia, my mother, and what it felt like to be somebody's daughter.

"Philadelphia—not even a small town," the doctor said, snapping a glove over his hand. "They knew better." He was telling me my mother was misinformed, that my mother had a bad doctor. Or worse, that I had a bad mother.

"Let's have a look," he said slicking his gloved hand with KY jelly. "Oh, you're a DES baby, alright," he announced, as if he was telling me something I hadn't known since I was 15 and my mother took me for my first pelvic exam. My mother told me she took a drug when she was pregnant that might cause problems. But if nothing showed up by the time I was 25, I'd be fine.

At the time, I had no idea what kind of "problems" she meant. I never asked. Later in life, I learned there was a high risk of uterine cancer. And recently, I understood that being a "DES baby" could mean I have an improperly shaped uterus. I might have difficulty getting pregnant or have problems maintaining a pregnancy. Or both. My mother never explained any of that to me. I guess because pregnancy seemed so far away.

"You're DES all right," the doctor said. "Alice!" he yelled, opening the door while I lay there staring at my knees. "Come in here! Look at the shape of her vaginal opening. It's like a head of broccoli." Picking up a mirror, he asked me, "Do you want to see?"

"No thanks," I said. I knew that looking might make

me feel better informed, involved, "at one" with my vagina. But I wouldn't do it with these two. They made me feel like a case study, not a woman trying to find her way back to her body.

When I got home, I looked up DES in my copy of *Our Bodies, Ourselves*. Although studies showed "conclusively" as early as 1953 that DES was ineffective in preventing miscarriage, the FDA didn't warn pregnant women against using it until 1971, after they proved it could cause cancer. I was born in 1960. Why did he make me feel so bad?

East Meets West

So far, my infertility has been treated by strictly Western practitioners. I've resisted going to see my herb doctor in Chinatown because I wasn't sure I wanted a bag of ingredients that I'd have to brew for three hours without being certain of its contents. I didn't want my child to suffer the way I did from DES damage. Someday, my daughter could be asked by her doctor, "Did you know if your mother ever went to one of those herb doctors that made her brew a tea that looked like it was made out of the side of a tree?"

"Yes!" she'll say.

"Big mistake!" he'll say, and then tell her she was born without a uterus.

Instead, I've been drinking herbs that I can identify in my copy of *Wise Woman Herbal for the Childbearing Year*. Red clover. Red raspberry. Nettle. These herbs are innocent yet balancing and are available in easy-to-use tea bags from my local health food store. I know a woman who had three colonics, practiced lunar conception (keeping a white light on while you're having sex during the days you are ovulating), and got pregnant. My other friends got drunk and had sex. That worked, too. Another swears by a psychic who, at her last session, told her to go home, get in the shower with her husband, and make love that night if they wanted a boy. *She's* pregnant.

My yoga teacher has been working with me on womb harmony. This involves a seated, heel-to-heel, yoga position that creates a circle of energy around the lower portion of my body. I need to do this because once, on one of my really bad days, I had this vision. My child and I are in Riverside Park. He's playing in the sand with his little friends, then runs over to me yelling "Mommy, Mommy!" wanting a smile, a juice box or a reassuring hug. Instead of providing refreshments and a snuggle, I drag him out of the park, twisted with jealousy that he gets to have lunch with his mommy and I don't.

The last time I had lunch with my mother was 11 years ago when I went home for Thanksgiving. As usual, my parents picked me up at the train station. I got off the train with a guy I'd met during the ride. If he and I kept walking at the same pace, my mother would think we were together. If I wasn't with this guy, my mother would later say, "Why not? He looked like a nice person."

I spotted my mother standing at the top of the escalator waving a tissue yelling, "Here she is!" as if other people in the train station were equally thrilled by my arrival. My train friend and I watched my mother patting her eyes dry, positioning herself—arms wide open at the top of the escalator—for my embrace.

"How long has it been since you've seen each other?" he asked.

"Four weeks." I said.

"Four weeks?" he asked. "Is she always this happy to see you?"

"Yes."

Once I got into the car, my mother wouldn't ask me any questions. Instead, while my father drove, she'd turn around to face me in the back seat and say, "O.K., GO!" At this point, I'd tell her about the guy I liked on the eleventh floor, the museums I'd been to with my friend Michael (yes, Mom—the gay one), or I'd warn her about a pair of $850 Manolo Blahnik boots I shipped to the house to save on tax.

"I didn't buy them, so don't have a heart attack," I said. "Phyllis (my boss) bought them for me instead of giving me a raise."

"Do you get dental insurance with this job?" my father jumped in.

"Dear, that is not the point," my mother interrupted, then turned back to me. "Keep going!"

My mother was so proud of me that, when the boots finally came to the house, she took the boots and the box (with the price tag still on it) and dragged them all over the neighborhood. She wanted to show the neighbors how fabulous her daughter was with her New York lifestyle.

The day after Thanksgiving, my mother and I went into town, like always, to see the Christmas decorations. Then I'd take the train back to New York after lunch. The menus in town had grown more sophisticated since I was eight and begged my mother to go to the Automat so that I could put two nickels in the metal glass box and pull out a corn muffin that was too big to ever finish. On this day, we ordered grilled vegetable sandwiches on sourdough baguettes. To save calories, I asked for mine without cheese. My mother, after hearing me order, did the same. Even as I got older, my mother was still one of my best friends. That was why I had to share my latest obsession with her.

Over the last year, I'd been immersing myself in a series of books written by a woman who channeled the spirit of an "entity" that was over a thousand years old. I was fascinated by all her revelations about the illusion of time and her perspective on souls of the departed hovering around us. It was my spiritual awakening and I had to share it with my mother. That very morning, Shirley

MacLaine had been on Oprah talking about her latest book, *Dancing in the Light*, a New Age primer on out-of-body and after-life experiences. I took this as a sign to bring up the subject of life after death with my mother.

"I want you to know," I told her after the waitress left us alone, "this is not all there is. I've been reading about the spiritual world, and the souls of those we love are still around us."

My mother said nothing so I kept talking. "I want you to know," I said, "that I still think about Grandmom Belle, and I used to love it when she and I made *kugels* together." It was important for me say that her mother was the grandparent that I'd felt the closest to. And that wasn't all.

"She knows we're here," I told my mother with confidence as I picked up my baguette. This made my mother cry.

"I don't know if I believe in any of this," she said. "But you are my daughter and I love you very much. And I believe that *you* believe this, so, I believe *you*."

I didn't want our lunch to get too bogged down with the mystery of dying. So, to make my mother laugh, I said, "Listen. I've been thinking. Before you die, do you think you could get some better jewelry? Something substantial. Sophisticated. None of these little rings and bracelets you've collected at craft fairs over the years. Do you know what Bulgari is? You're 56 years old," I told her. "You deserve it."

Trying

On the way back to the train station, we went to a bookstore. I bought her a copy of Shirley MacLaine's book. My mother promised to read it. She even bought me a copy so we could talk about it together. As always, leaving was never "Goodbye." It was, "When are you coming in again?"

One month later, she was dead. I was handed an envelope with my mother's name on it. In the envelope was her wallet, photographs of our family, a note I had written to her on Mother's Day, and some of her jewelry. I don't think I'd have ever believed my mother was gone if not for the smell of smoke and the ashes left on her engagement ring. It was the jewelry I'd seen on her hands for 25 years. Every once in a while, like the day of my wedding, I take out her tiny necklace—the one with a gold initial for her name, and wear it.

East Versus West

The trouble I'm having trying to be holistic about my infertility is that the more I see my problem as a physical one—my increasingly high FSH—the less meditation seems to help. It wasn't a matter of making my womb send a happy message to the sperm and visualizing a few of them doing the Olympic 50-meter freestyle through my cervix to my egg. Oliver's sperm had trouble reaching their destination because of blockages, and those that made it through couldn't connect because of the quality of my eggs. No mantra in the world would change that, or could it?

IVF would be the normal next course. But there was a six-month wait-list for the procedure, and the doctors here didn't exactly love me because my chances of success weren't promising. Although my FSH level was considered "borderline," Dr. I-Can't-Believe-Your-Mother-Took-DES suggested a round of drug therapy to see how well I'd react to having my egg production stimulated. Another test. Another grade. Another reason to feel bad about my body.

Keeping positive is hard. I'm tired of going to yoga. Every week, I avoid the inverted poses—the ones you're not supposed to do when you are menstruating. I was sure my instructor was thinking, "Barbara's not pregnant yet." The other day, a woman at my gym called to me from the treadmill as she worked off her postpartum bulge. She knew I was trying. Even offered me her leftover ovulation sticks because she wouldn't need them anymore. And since then, not a week goes by that she doesn't ask me if I'm pregnant.

One time, she yelled, "Any luck?" across the training floor. "Not yet," I said, giving her a tortured smile. No. No luck. I'm unlucky. Would you like to hear how my life has been going so far? I hate people.

"Don't work out too hard," another friend warned, as I cycled away my stress. "You look thin. Are you eating?" They make me think I don't want a baby badly enough.

Trying

I went to Barnes and Noble to read up on exercising and pregnancy. In my neighborhood, the "How To" books on pregnancy are right next to the children's section. I have to walk through a sea of mothers who have parked their strollers and are seated in the aisles reading, "Hop on Pop" to their kids, then go around the corner to look for the how-to books on pregnancy. I'm afraid of being seen by someone I know—especially a mother, and especially one who had no trouble getting pregnant. Motherhood may be just around the corner, but watching the other parents with kids old enough to read makes me feel like it's a lifetime away.

Every book I read says that exercise is good for toning the reproductive organs, and that keeping in shape is good mentally and physically. However, I avoid breaking into a sweat on the days when Oliver and I just tried, and I make sure my pulse stays lower that 140 beats per minute. Trust me. There are days when I don't even feel my heart beating.

Oddly enough, for someone who works out as a way to stay sane, I haven't been to the gym in weeks. I have an injury. I severely sprained my psoas muscle—another part of my body I never heard of until I learned it was damaged. The psoas is a long, thick muscle that basically connects the lower back to the thighs. I've been going to see my yoga instructor, who's also my massage therapist, for treatment. I told her that I thought my injury might be a response to the surgery I'd been through, and more specifically, a result of the treatment I got from my *ex-gynecologist*. She agreed. My other theory is that, on the day of the injury, I was at the gym doing a lateral-pull with a 40-pound weight over my right shoulder when in walks this guy who looks very much like Oliver. We'd spoken a few times. Once, we even stood next to each other in a yoga class and my instructor couldn't get over how much he looked like my husband. He's tall, blond, cute, and has the same deep voice as Oliver. In fact, he did voice-over work and I'd heard he was also a stand-up comic. That sounded like fun! Was I married when I first met this guy or merely engaged? Did I marry the wrong blond? At that moment, I felt a tear in my lower back.

The Follicular Phase

My period came. No big surprise. In fact, oddly enough, I'm happy because now I have something to do. I have to go for another "day 3" FSH blood test and a sonogram. Afterward, they'll give me a "challenge" test to see if my body responds well to fertility drugs. If it does, it means in vitro fertilization is not out of the question.

All of these tests feel like Chinese water torture—one drop a day until they'll finally tell me what I have instinctively known all my life: I won't be able to conceive a child.

"You just say you 'know' you won't be able to conceive

so that you can feel in control," my therapist told me when I first started trying.

"No," I told her. "I say these things because this is how I think life works for me." I've always thought I had strong instincts. They give me a sense of order, even if I hate the outcome. Is this instinct, or me just not being able to imagine something? Instincts and fears are indistinguishable when you're watching your fate unfold in a doctor's office.

When I was in my early twenties, I remember telling my mother, "Don't wait for me to have grandchildren." What did I mean by that? That I would never be able to *have* children or that she wouldn't be alive to *see* them? Maybe it's good that she's gone. Not good that she's dead, but good because maybe it means that I could still *have* them. That's it. Whew! I can still have children.

Nervous, but excited, I took a deep breath, breezed through the doctor's office door and signed the registration. I grabbed the pamphlet entitled, "Infertility: The Emotional Roller Coaster," stuffed it into my pocketbook, and waited. I watched as other women entered and then greeted the receptionist by name. They'd been coming here longer than I had. They're in the program. I'd get to know all the receptionists too—if I'm lucky.

Inside the examining room, I pulled out the pamphlet. Under the "Myths of Infertility" section, it reads, "Our experience teaches us that hard work pays off. But infertility has nothing to do with effort. It is scientific." Translation: It's not my fault. Yes it is. I should have slept with Joel Seidelman when I was 19 years old. Joel wasn't my first boyfriend. He was my first love. We met one summer when we were both counselors at Camp Akiba. I met him the first night of orientation when we stood up on High Hill and he showed me the stars. After only three days, we were falling in love and doing the "Ear Thing" at the same spot.

"Would you do something for me?" Joel asked.

"Like what?" I said.

"Would you scream into my ear?" he asked.

"What?"

"Yell, for a few seconds, into my ear. Here, I'll show you," he said.

Joel cupped his hand over my right ear and braced my head with his other hand. Slowly, he released this "UHHHHHHHH" noise into my ear. It immediately tickled. A warm sensation penetrated my entire body. Gradually, he intensified this vibration until I shook with laughter. When he finally stopped, the instant relief created a final rush. *That* was the Ear Thing.

Joel was tall (important for my five-foot, nine-inch frame), had broad shoulders, strong arms, and lots of chest hair. I could see the hair creeping out of his T-shirts, in colors that, like Joel, were intense. Red, purple and black, with logos of groups like Led Zeppelin. I loved the way my head fit into his chest. Lying on his bed, clothes on, we talked for hours. Soothed by the smell of his freshly laundered shirt, I had never felt safer.

I told Joel about what had happened in my family the winter before. My father had undergone brain surgery. I told Joel about the way the surgery had left my father looking bald, fragile and old. And how, for the very first time, I thought about what it would be like to go through life without my father. Joel reached over to kiss me and his face was soaked with tears. I had never had the courage to cry.

Part of me wanted to sleep with Joel. But Joel had this way of discussing sex as if it were a course I should be taking next semester. "I'm not just saying this, Barb," he said. "But I think I would be a very good person for you to sleep with for your first time." I couldn't. Not until I conferred with my best friend who was working at another overnight camp. She'd already done it. She'd let me know what I was supposed to feel when it was right. I'd wait to talk to her.

The summer ended, we returned home, and my relationship with Joel was no longer about midnight meetings after "lights out." It became weekend dates and late-night phone calls. I loved the sound of his voice—strong, but with a soothing resonance. I could hear his lips ending every word with a smile. Joel made me do the Ear Thing over the phone. I'd have to put the receiver under my pillow so my parents, asleep in the next room, wouldn't think I was in agony.

My mother was very supportive. "If you really like Joel," she said, "let me know and we'll go and we'll get a diaphragm." Then, on the night of my twentieth birthday, he comes over to pick me up. And before we leave, my mother drags me into our den and says, "I just want to know. Does he *own* a dinner jacket?"

So, Mr. First-Sexual-Experience got dumped because he didn't have the appropriate dinner jacket. I started to see Joel through my mother's eyes and decided he wasn't quite good enough for me.

I broke up with him because, well, I could tell you a story about not wanting to marry Joel because then I'd have to move to a small town in upstate Pennsylvania and I could never be happy there. But I know better now. I didn't sleep with Joel because I was scared. Maybe if I *had* slept with Joel, I wouldn't have needed to remain single for so many years after my parents' death. I purposely dated men I had no intention of marrying. If only I'd allowed myself the closeness of a real relationship with Joel, I'd have lost my virginity years sooner and embraced my body instead of starving it. I'd have had a few more relationships by my late twenties, been married by 30, and I'd still have eggs left. I hate myself for walking out of Joel's bedroom that night. Have I mentioned that obsessing is a symptom of infertility?

Finally, after staring at a Thomas McKnight print of a sunset in Santa Fe for as long as I could stand it, the doctor came in. I watched him put a condom over the sonogram wand, lubricate it, and put the wand inside of me. I was getting slightly used to this method of seeing inside my uterus. But if you've never gone through it, imagine someone putting a stick-shift deep inside you and moving from second gear into reverse, two or three times.

The doctor showed me the image of my ovaries in the monitor. I stared into what looked like a black and white television monitor filled with static until I saw two dark masses—one on the right and one on the left. I wanted to let him know I was interested, so I said something profound like, "Uh-huh." He told me that someone would be calling me that night with my drug instructions.

On the way out, a nurse handed me a tape entitled, "Fertinex: Your Video Guide to Reconstitution and Administration." I was psyched to be trying something new. The plan was this: if the drugs helped me produce more eggs, Oliver and I would do an insemination that month. Oliver would bring his sperm to the doctor's office where they'd wash and count them. Then I'd lie on an examining table while the doctor used an instrument to directly inject the sperm through my cervix. You can stimulate eggs without undergoing an insemination. But if you're going through all the shots, you might as well have clean sperm and a direct insertion.

This might just work! I could get pregnant. All without my mother. Until now, I could never imagine having a baby without my mother. But beginning our first fertility treatment has propelled me into a new reality. None of the things I'm doing to get pregnant—the injections, the surgeries, the technology—has anything to do with my mother or what she may have experienced when she got pregnant. I'm sure she had her share of humiliating examinations, but the advances in fertility treatments belong to my generation. And while I focus on the science and hope for success, I forget to miss my mother.

I've been trying to imagine what pregnancy would feel like. A mound of flesh extending from my body—something inside of me that I'd be guarding for nine months. But my baby is also a separate part. There will be a cord. We will share blood and nourishment. But inside my womb will be this other person. I promise myself, for now and for the rest of my life, to remember the boundaries.

Injecting My Thigh

On the night I gave myself my first injection of pure FSH—follicle stimulating hormone extracted from the urine of post-menopausal women—I wondered about the woman responsible for my particular vial. Who was she? What did she look like?

The morning after, my thighs looked thinner. I wondered if *she* had anything to do with it. Perhaps she was one of those active, older women. The type you see on prune juice commercials who swims 30 laps a day at her home in Southern California. No. The doctors probably gave me urine from an *East* Coast post-menopausal woman. Maybe she was from the Hamptons. Southampton, I hoped. I didn't want any of those glittery eye-shadowed women from West Hampton. Actually, I preferred East Hampton. A lot of artists live there. No, Amagansett. I wanted old money.

After watching the instruction video, I didn't feel any better about giving myself an injection. First of all, the woman in the video was fat. When she prepped her thighs for the needle, there was no risk of hitting anything other than puffy, fatty flesh. I was worried about sticking a muscle and watching my blood fill up the vial. They taught you how to check for this on the outside chance that it could happen. Just thinking about it made me lightheaded.

The first thing I had to do was make my night table germ-free. That involved clearing away five months of unread magazines, coffee stains and half a cookie. Then I washed my hands with anti-bacterial soap, opened up the first of several sterilized pads, and picked up the first vial of medication.

Opening up the vial requires breaking a stem of glass that only comes off if you pull the stem when the little blue dot, imprinted on the glass, is facing *in*. I pick it up. Wait! Did they say facing in, or facing out? I fill my first vial of powder with distilled water—no problem.

The second one, I almost dropped. That's when Oliver reminded me they cost $50 a pop.

"Maybe you should leave," I told him, as I nervously lined up the vial and water. "Do you think you should leave?"

"If you'll feel more comfortable with me leaving, I'll leave," he said.

"No, you better not." I said. If something went wrong, I wanted it to be both our faults.

Filling the vials with water and watching the crystals dissolve into a serum brought back memories of my brother's chemistry set. We used to collect crickets from under our cellar steps, mix up a potion, drop the crickets in and see how they'd react. David is three years older than I am. He taught me the finer things in life—like spitting for distance and the names of the players in the American and National Baseball Leagues. When my parents took us along to a certain antique store where children weren't welcome, we'd stand out front, make faces through the windows, then pretend to beat each other up until one of them came out.

Growing up, I used to feel badly for people who didn't have an older brother. Later on was a different story. I'm not like my brother. I've made very different choices. And over the years, there were times we had a hard time understanding each other.

David has two children—a boy and a girl. Before each child was born, I remember my brother telling me that he hit a "bull's-eye" their very first month of trying. I was just praying I could hit my thigh with this needle. But first, I had to draw the liquid out of the bottle into the needle. I adjusted the nightstand light so I could see the needle better. There was dust on the lamp. Does this mean I have to go back and sterilize my hands? I'd better.

The liquid hormone adheres to the bottom of the vial, so you have to find the side of the needle that has a tiny hole in its tip, and put that tip into a puddle of fluid the size of a drop of water. Then you pull back on the plunger—*but not too far*. After repeating this procedure three times, I opened the bottle of alcohol to wash down my leg. I stroked the saturated pad along my thigh, searching for a welcoming spot. I pulled my skin together to ready it for the subcutaneous injection. It looked like a grapefruit. Oh my God! Is this cellulite?

"I can't do it," I told Oliver. I'd gotten so immersed in the preparation that I completely forgot that it was all leading up to the injection. I need to stab myself in the leg "like a dart," as Nurse Alice described. I envisioned the dartboard my brother and I played with in the basement of our old house. It had colored rings on one side and a baseball diamond on the other. I looked at my innocent thigh. I apologized for the injection it was about to receive, and plunged in.

The nurse was right. I felt nothing but a slight prick, but it was shocking to see my hand on a needle sticking into my thigh. I still had to push it a little deeper for it to be completely inside. I know that, for diabetics, injections are a way of life. And the needle I was using was only one-half of an inch long. But as a first-timer, it felt like six. I released my skin and pushed the plunger down to inject the medication.

"Now what?" I asked Oliver, while still holding the needle.

"Keep your skin *raised* while pressing down on the plunger," he read from the instructions.

"Uh–oh. I already pushed the plunger and my skin is relaxed!" I told him.

"You didn't!"

"I did." Then I pulled the needle out.

"Then, while your skin is *raised*," he continued, "remove the needle."

"I already removed the needle."

"What? You should've asked me what to do next. You're always doing things in such a hurry," he yelled.

"You expect me to push the needle into my skin and hold it there while I turn to look at you for further instruction? *You* try having a needle in your leg. See if *you* go slowly."

He probably would.

After two nights of injections, it was time to return to the office to have my ovaries checked. If the eggs look like they are maturing properly and have reached the point in my cycle where they need to be released, you go to phase two—the HCG shot. This is the big gun—literally. Or, at least, the big needle. HCG, or human chorionic gonadotropin, is a hormone that increases the levels of progesterone and helps stimulate ovulation in women. The drug is suspended in a heavy oil, like sesame. You have to use a large needle to draw the drug out of the vial, then disconnect it from the syringe and replace it with another needle, which is thinner. This is the needle that gets stuck into my rear end.

"You can have your husband do it, or you can come to the office," the nurse told us.

"No, my husband loves this kind of thing. We got it covered."

Oliver was into it. We lined up everything on the dresser. While standing in position—arms on table, rear end protruding—I tried to stay calm while simultaneously bracing myself for the shot. I had no idea how much pain to expect.

"Are you ready?" Oliver asked.

"Don't ask me if I'm ready! If you ask me if I am ready, I'll get tense."

"O.K.," he said. "Sorry." And he truly was. For all of it.

Then I felt this Poi–n–n–g! as the needle attempted to go into my skin but bounced off instead.

"What the hell was that?" I yelled, yanking my head around to see.

It was only then that I allowed myself to look at the

needle. Jesus, it was big. Too big! Mr. "Medical Journalist" had forgotten to switch the needle.

Before The Morning After

"Do you want to be alone?" I asked. "Or should I help you get started?"

"Alone."

"O.K." I said. "I'll be in the other room." I grabbed my makeup bag off the dresser and walked toward the door.

"You're putting on makeup to be inseminated?" Oliver yelled from his position on the bed.

"I'm getting my haircut after," I said. I would have put on makeup even if I wasn't. These days, I make sure my toes are polished for every sonogram.

After what seemed like enough time, I gently walked by our bedroom door.

"Why don't you just come in here?" he asked.

I did, and we were actually having some fun. So much fun that Oliver entrusted me with the specimen cup. At the big moment, I'd have to slip it over the head of his penis to "catch" the product. That maneuver was like trying to put a cup over a small scampering animal. My hand shook more than he did. We cracked up and I left the room.

Eventually, Oliver emerged from the room with the cup in hand.

Trying

"Nice job," was all I said, as we ran downstairs to a catch a cab to the doctor's office.

While we waited for Oliver's sperm to be prepped, we went to a diner around the corner from the doctor's office and talked about how trying had become much more than figuring out which day I ovulated. It hadn't been that long ago that we were imagining how nice it'd be to have a baby in May or June, or reading books on how to increase your chances of having a boy or a girl. But here we were, having omelets in an unfamiliar East Side diner, waiting for our next round of hope.

"Do you want your husband to be with you during the procedure?" the nurse asked, as she walked me to the exam room. Amazingly, I never considered that a possibility. I was so used to feeling that what I was going through was all about what doctors do to *me*, I never thought of an insemination as being the moment of conception and that *we* should be together.

"Yes, please," I answered back. Be polite. If you're polite, they'll like you. And if they like you, they'll try harder to make it work.

As I lay back on the table, the doctor asked me if I was ready. Next, he looked over at Oliver, which I liked, then pushed a syringe filled with sperm straight through my cervix. I looked over at Oliver and smiled. The same way I did when we were under our wedding *chuppah*. The "I'm so happy, but this is *so* strange" kind of look.

Everyone who meets Oliver understands how it

could be that, with all my religious upbringing, I could marry someone out of my faith. We came from different religions—Oliver was raised Roman Catholic. But our sense of family life was exactly the same. My friends loved him immediately. Until I met Oliver, I was always the prize in the relationship. My friends would take any new boyfriend aside and say, "Treat her well. You're lucky to have her." When Oliver came into my life, my friends pulled *me* aside to say, "He's great! Have you made him nuts yet?"

We had a Jewish wedding and spent a lot of time working on our ceremony to incorporate the traditions of our two backgrounds. The rabbi who married us was a woman, and our friends and family came from all religions and lifestyles—our own cultural melting pot. Everyone seemed happy with our union until Oliver's cousin from Düsseldorf got up and gave a toast in both German and English. Immediately after, my mother's friend, Marsha pulled me away from my first bite of poached salmon in dill sauce to say, "You told me you were marrying somebody who wasn't Jewish. But you never told me he was a German!"

Before the doctor left the examination room, he told me I should rest for 10 to 15 minutes and said, "Now it's up to science."

"Or God," I remember thinking.

Oliver jumped out of his seat as soon as the door closed and said, "I have to kiss you."

Trying

* * *

By the time the nurse came to tell us we could go home, I was reading aloud from *Time Out Magazine*'s list of the best hamburgers in New York City. On my way out of the office, Nurse Alice told me I'm on the "list," which meant that, even if the insemination failed, I was officially in line for an IVF cycle sometime between January and April. Yes!

The Luteal Phase

It's the days between ovulation and my period when I build false hope. One day, I awoke feeling lightheaded. While sitting at my computer, I began to feel nauseated. My keyboard seemed to float and I felt lightheaded as I wrote. I couldn't focus my eyes on the screen. Is this it? Is this what being pregnant feels like?

I took a few walks around the house thinking, wondering, getting slightly excited. Then I remembered. The night before, Oliver and I had been on a boat ride around Manhattan. I didn't feel sick then, but I do remember being very cold and thinking that this three-hour tour was taking closer to five. I'd never experienced it before, but maybe the movement of the water was still in me. Perhaps I was suffering from residual seasickness. Damn.

My workday became a total waste. All morning, a plumber had been working on our bathroom pipes. A leak from our neighbors upstairs had turned our wall and ceiling into a wet saltine. The plumber couldn't tell if the damage was from my neighbors overflowing their bathtub, or if the building had bad pipes. This would make the third time in six months that they tore open our walls without solving the problem. The plumber suggested pouring a dye into the upstairs bathtub to reveal where the leak originated.

Thinking about dyes and plumbing made me cringe. I needed to leave the apartment while they worked. Oliver, on the other hand, gets very involved in talking to plumbers. It reminds him of being a real homeowner, which we're not. We're only renting.

I've started to think about adoption. The night before, my favorite medical drama had a story about a woman making peace with her choice to adopt. How *choice* is the empowering thing, not just whether, as women, we use our bodies to deliver the baby. We are still empowered to choose a life. It was the third show I happened to see that week about adoption. It's just like the song on the radio you think was written for you. I took these coincidences as God's way of breaking it to me: I'd have to adopt.

I wondered if my infertility was all part of God's master plan—me not being able to give birth to my own flesh and blood to spare me the pain of seeing my parents' faces in the faces of my children. That would feel like the ultimate separation. Is this what I get for being too close to my parents?

Trying

When my friends ask me for my fertility update, I don't know what to tell them. I don't want to alienate them by saying too little, and I don't want to tell them more than I feel comfortable telling them. But, somehow, my comfort level takes a back seat to their need to know. I'm sure they think they're helping.

"It's not that bad," I tell them. "I've seen hell already and, believe me, this isn't it." It's true. I'd been through worse. This wasn't death. This was just a part of my life that was taking longer than I'd expected.

I hear stories of women who break down into a crying heap on the floor every month they get their period. I tell myself that, for these women, infertility might be the worst thing that has ever happened to them. They may never have had their lives turned inside out by loss. I must be strong. I have to be. I'm afraid of ever feeling that sad about anything ever again.

A part of me still believes that my problem is that I can't visualize myself *having* a child. I've been so busy bracing myself for the fall of *not* having a child, that I have deprived myself—my body—of the image of motherhood. Now, when I go to sleep, instead of reviewing the first 36 years of my life, I try to picture what a child of Oliver's and mine might look like—his blond hair, my curls, both of our long legs. If we had a girl and she had small breasts, that would be because of me. Would I tell her what my mother told me when she sensed I was waiting for my bustline to arrive?

"You're not going to have large breasts," my mother told me. "I don't have them, so you won't. And I don't want you waiting around only to be disappointed."

When I was younger, I'd decided I could tell that my bust had reached grown-up proportion if, while wearing a shirt, I could successfully balance a book on my chest. Never happened. But I'm O.K. with my breasts. I like not having to wear a bra, and not worrying that when I get older, the only thing separating my chest from my waist might be a belt. I wonder if my mother's breasts were a big disappointment to her? My mother also had fat calves—actually, fat thighs. They were her greatest physical disappointment. "Thank God you don't have my legs," she'd say. "You're lucky. You're built like Flossie."

Flossie was my mother's best friend. My mother used Flossie as her reference for someone tall and thin, and she loved telling me how graceful Flossie looked as she got older. At five foot nine, I was taller than my mother by three inches. My father was 5'10"—only an inch taller than I was. I figured I got my height from my grandfather. He had been over six feet tall. Perhaps it was because Flossie was a woman, and that I, uncomfortable with my height all during high school, needed a role model, even if it was a person I'm not related to.

Truth is, I might have been built like someone I never met—my father's mother, Anna. My Grandmom Ida was really my *step*-grandmother, a fact I didn't learn until I was 19. I was with my parents, sitting in the back seat of our car, on the way to see my brother's first apartment. I don't remember what we were talking about, but it was something heated enough that my mother became annoyed that my father wasn't expressing his emotions. She mumbled something to him about, "exhibiting a behavior he might have gotten from the orphanage."

"What orphanage?" I piped in, suddenly finding the conversation to be of immense interest.

"Well," my mother began, uncomfortably. "You know that Grandmom Ida isn't really . . . well, she *is* your grandmother. Nobody could have been a better grandmother to you kids. When you were young, she was very helpful to me the way she used to cook for you and drive herself over when you were sick. She *is* your grandmother, so don't think any differently."

"O.K. O.K.," I said. "But what about the orphanage?"

"You knew that Daddy's real mother died when he was a baby, didn't you?"

"NO."

"Well, we don't like to talk about it," she whispered.

"There's no one else in the car!" I said.

I cornered my brother the minute we got to his new home. "Did you know Grandmom Ida isn't Daddy's real mother?"

"Sort of," he said.

"How can you *sort of* know? And you knew that Daddy lived in an orphanage with Uncle Norman until he was three?"

Turns out, my father's mother died when he was three months old. Until my grandfather remarried, the two brothers lived in the Jewish Home for Children. I'm still processing what that must have meant for my father, living without either of his parents in a strange place, then learning—years later—that his real mother had died.

We never talked about his early years, but it might have explained why my father was the silent type. Sure, Sy Nuddle was the toastmaster at weddings and quite the bon vivant around my friends. I was the girl with the cool dad, the dad who took Debbie Brown and me to ice hockey games and rock concerts when we were too young to drive. But my father kept his feelings inside. Throughout his life and through several operations, my father was a stoic. I attribute all of my "internal fortitude" (that's exactly how he would have put it) to my father. Whenever I was confused about life or frustrated with school, he'd tell me, "In the immortal words of a great prophet, 'This too shall pass.'" He never told me how.

By day, I am strong. By night, I feel viscerally cut off from my family—like a tree with dying roots and no hope of growing any more branches. Truncated. Stuck. Stumped. I want more family, yet no one is coming.

Chapter Two

I'm not pregnant—period.

It's day 27 of my cycle and I've started to stain. No, bleed. If I say "staining," I can make myself believe it won't last. I've heard stories of pregnant women who stained in their first month. It has something to do with the embryo attaching itself to the uterus. Maybe that's what was happening to me. Yeah, right. But I knew differently. The truth seeped in like the wetness between my legs. My mind raced back to the day of the insemination when I was on the precipice of "what if" and everything seemed possible. Then my thoughts came crashing back. Shit. My body is back on empty. Less than empty. Because now I can't DO anything for at least another month. The doctors make you skip a month to let your body calm down from the effects of the follicle stimulating drugs. Let's just see how much calmer I get before this month is over.

I wasn't sure exactly what the next step was, so I called the doctor's office. I made certain to leave my message for the doctor that I liked and NOT the doctor who mentioned my name every third word in a sentence. He, too, was skeptical about my chances of ever becoming pregnant, but at least he seemed more sympathetic.

"Well, that's bad news," he said, after I told him I'd gotten my period. Could we stop stating the obvious for one minute and say something, anything, to make me feel better? Then he said, "Let me take another look at your chart." I imagined him holding the receiver, waiting the obligatory amount of time on the phone while pretending to fully examine my chart.

For years, I worked on Seventh Avenue as a salesperson in a showroom. Every so often, a shop owner would call me, desperate for an already sold-out sweater. "Barb, please," she'd beg. "My best customer is leaving on a cruise and they absolutely have to have the pineapple sweater that goes with the pineapple print pant."

I'd say, "I hate to tell you this, but we're sold out."

Then she'd say, "Barb, you don't understand. The customer is right here, standing at the register, ready to buy the whole outfit if I could only find her the sweater."

These women don't want to hear that there was really

nothing I could do. So, I'd tell them, "You know what? Hold on a moment. I'll look in the back."

There was no back.

I'm on to you Doctor Who-Thinks-I-Have-Little-or-No-Chance-of-Conceiving. Just get back on the phone. Let me hear you come back to me with some real news.

"Well, your husband has great sperm, wonderful sperm," he said, returning to the phone. "You—with your high FSH—you might need to use donor eggs."

Excuse me? DONOR eggs??? It amazes me that these doctors can just slip in the idea of using another woman's eggs, another woman's GENES, and mixing them with my husband's sperm to make our child, with absolutely no warning or sensitivity. I was stunned.

Now I *longed* to hear my name. Now I wanted to hear a doctor say, "Barbara, we understand that you want to conceive a child. It's just that, Barbara, your eggs may not be good enough. We're sorry, Barbara. It's not your fault, Barbara. You, Barbara, did nothing wrong. And you were right not to have married Jonathan Dansky when you were 28 just so you could conceive a child. We don't think you're the Great Neck type, either, and we applaud you for saying no."

Sometimes

The first time my mother came to me in a dream, she was wearing a chiffon scarf and cat's-eye sunglasses. I watched her as she floated over my neighbor's house and then into my backyard. My mother hovered at a distance close enough for me to see her face, but far enough away that I couldn't look into her eyes. I so wished she would come closer, but I didn't dare ask her for fear that she would leave.

"Mom!" I shouted. "Hi! This is great! Tell me, what should I do about Jonathan?"

I'd been dating Jonathan Dansky for the past six months. We had nothing in common. It was the year after losing my parents and I had already been through my New Age Crystal Enlightenment phase, been toying with Buddhism, and had thrown out seven copies of *When Bad Things Happen to Good People*. I thought it might be a good idea if I dated—possibly married—a nice Jewish boy from Long Island. He was a lawyer and he took me to a lot of black-tie events. I got to get dressed-up a lot and pretend to be happy.

I'd wanted to break up with him, but couldn't. And now, here comes my mother to tell me what to do. I don't even remember *what* she said, because when you dream about someone who's dead, they don't necessarily speak to you in words. They speak to you heart-to-heart. It was like hearing the absolute truth for the very first time. You couldn't possibly repeat it to someone else. But to me, it meant something. And then I said, "Mom. This is great! We could do this every week. How about Thursdays?"

And she said, "No! I won't come to you every time you ask. Only sometimes."

Her face dissolved into a wake of chiffon as she drifted out of my backyard and into the sky. I was so pissed off that the next day, while cleaning my apartment, I accidentally threw out her diamond stud earrings. It was not long after that I broke up with Jonathan.

My doctor kept talking. "Do you know anyone 30 years old or under? You could use *their* eggs." Eggs? Someone else's? Younger? Let me just check the dairy section at the Food Emporium for a carton with a later expiration date and I'll get back to you!

I couldn't wait to tell all of this to my best friend, Jeptha, who immediately offered me her eggs, as a joke. "Guess what," I told her. "You're 37. You're too old!" I wanted her to feel that sting. I needed her to understand what it feels like for me, and for other women, to be told—with the compassion of an overworked waitress—that they may be out of eggs.

I met Jeptha at a fashion trade show in Atlanta. You weren't just a salesperson at these trade shows, you were a waitress; offering to bring customers the walnut chicken salad or the cold poached salmon before showing them row after row of multiple striped T-shirts. After a few hours of this, I took leave from my booth and raced to grab a cup of coffee. I squatted in the corner of the showroom, balancing my coffee in one hand while opening my Chanel compact to quickly reapply lipstick before returning to the next round of customers. Across the room, I noticed another salesperson doing the exact same thing. I waited for her to take a sip from her coffee and when she looked up, I shouted, "Do you have a life?"

"No." she said.

"Me neither," I said walking over. When she stood up, I realized we were the same height. In fact, she was slightly taller. She had blond, spiky hair, lots of arm bracelets, and was, as I soon learned, very adventurous. Jeptha moved out of her house when she was 16, ran her own restaurant when she was 19 and, as she says, "got in some trouble down South." At 20, she moved to New York to pay off her debts. While we talked, we devoured these dark chocolate business cards that were provided by the showroom owner.

Before racing back to our booths, I asked, "When we get back to New York, would you like to have dinner sometime?"

"Yes," she said. "But let's really do it. Let's not be like those people who'll say they'll have lunch and then don't."

Back in New York, we shared expensive meals, sent each other flowers after our respective bad dates, and dashed out of our showrooms for quick sanity checks on the corner of Seventh Avenue and 38th.

After my parents died, we'd talk about life and how we weren't living the lives we wanted. Jeptha longed to move back to the mountains where she grew up. She wanted to get married and have a child. I wanted I didn't know what: an adventure, a master's degree, certification as a yoga instructor—something, anything that didn't resemble the "normal" life I could no longer have. In some ways, we both got what we wanted.

After a few moments of phone silence—I think my doctor was beginning to sense my shock—he changed the subject. He admitted that during my last round of stimulation, I responded surprisingly well to the drugs.

"I'd have never known you had such a high FSH level judging by your response. We could consider increasing the dosage the next time."

Well *that's* good. After six months of feeling let down by my body, I can finally feel like I did something right. I proved that my body could receive pure hormone, which I have carefully and efficiently learned how to inject into my thigh, and produce more eggs. The question is: how good are the eggs?

What was I thinking by waiting so long to get pregnant? I'll tell you what I was thinking. I was thinking that plenty of women get pregnant when they're in their thirties, with or without assisted reproductive technology. In one week, I'll turn 37. O.K., so I won't get to tell my husband that I'm pregnant on my birthday. Instead, I found out that I need to have another hysteroscopy—my second—to remove some more fibroids in my uterus that showed up on my last sonogram. This time, it's done as an office procedure while I'm numbed, but awake. I can watch the whole thing on a monitor. It's very Discovery Channel. Jesse, the receptionist, called to tell me when the operation was scheduled. I told her that it happened to be the same day as my birthday, but a cake wouldn't be necessary.

The Chi of Life

I've decided to leave the test tubes behind and move on to ovulation sticks—much easier. You just pee onto the absorbent tip and the result comes up in five minutes. A blue line means you're having an LH surge (luteinizing hormone is the chemical your body produces that lets you know when you are about to ovulate). No line means it's too soon in your cycle, or you've completely missed your chance. After nine days, when I should have been ovulating, I couldn't detect a surge. Was my recent surgery throwing my cycle off? Or was my cycle confused by the herbs I'd been taking from my acupuncturist? I'd recently gone to her for my second session.

"Have you been taking the herbs?" she asked, examining my palm. She'd given me a special powdered drink to prepare my system for conception.

"Well, I took them for three days, then stopped. You told me to *stop* taking herbs right before I was going to try to conceive."

Trying

"You're *trying* this month?" she asked. "Stick out your tongue." In Chinese medicine, the tongue is like a map of the body.

"Why?" I asked, in between tongue extensions. "Shouldn't I be trying?"

(That's why I'm here. I have sex and you make it stick.)

"I thought you'd skip this month so that you could do the herbs," she said matter-of-factly.

What is she talking about? She never told me not to try this month. Besides, she doesn't understand what skipping a month means. It means I lose a chance to say I conceived naturally—without drugs, and without having to spend thousands of dollars for in vitro fertilization. I could go to an acupuncturist 10 times and it would be one-twentieth the cost of IVF. Oliver and I could take a vacation; return to that villa in Italy and eat linguini *a la vongole* at that little bistro under the steps of the church in Amalfi.

When I really let myself think about it—to feel what is going on—I realize it isn't the money that keeps me praying the natural method will work. It's the allure of the normal. Just *once* I'd like to have a major life event occur without the bittersweet taste of knowing what was sacrificed. Lying on the table with 27 very fine needles stuck into my body to balance my energy, I felt trapped between East and West. I wanted the herbs. I needed the drugs. And I prayed to God to let me get pregnant without either.

I can't remember what it feels like not to try. Is that the point? Holistically speaking, is it better to skip a month so Oliver and I could remember what it's like to have sex because we want to, and not because the ovulation indicator says we *have* to? Too late. Sex is a means to an end right now. Trying to remember otherwise—when sex was tender, lingering, or passionate—is like switching the channel on a television that no longer gets regular reception. We need the cable box.

Besides, I need to try. I need to keep the process going. My life has become a circus act, the one I saw as a kid on *The Ed Sullivan Show* where this guy runs back and forth spinning several plates on sticks, trying to keep them all up in the air. These days, I'm running from one remedy to the next; massaging this, ingesting that, acupuncturing this, inseminating that. If I slow down, I'll break the rhythm of possibility. As for Oliver, he'd freak if I told him the acupuncturist suggested we don't try this month because an herbalist said so. Yet, I'd already skipped a month because my Western doctor told me to. Should I be going East or West?

I've been re-reading my feng shui book. Feng Shui, the Chinese art of living in harmony with your environment, uses a chart that refers to the eight basic building blocks from the *I Ching*, called trigrams. Each trigram is associated with specific treasures in life, such as health, wealth, love or fertility.

My bedroom is located in the wealth and prosperity

trigram. Good. And we have very good sheets, too. I was glad Oliver and I decided not to stay in a hotel on our wedding night and chose, instead, to spend the cost of a wedding suite at the Pierre on high-thread-count European sheets. After the wedding, I went back to the store to get an extra set, and the sales woman showed me one that was even more expensive than what we already owned. Not wanting to act like I couldn't afford it, I decided to use my husband as an excuse. I told the salesperson, "I'll have to check with the person I live with, er . . . I mean my partner." She continued to pull out her fall line of Egyptian cottons. I needed to stop her. "Really," I said. I want to come back with my, uh . . ."

Finally, the woman said, "I see. Why don't you bring her by the next time you come." Her? Back then, I felt uncomfortable using the word, "husband" because it meant I had become somebody's "wife." It all felt so predictable, so boring. Now I worry that, despite all our efforts, I still have trouble accepting the concept that I might become somebody's "mommy."

According to the principles of feng shui, my bathrooms, located in the center back of our apartment, are in between the "Wealth and Prosperity" and "Love and Marriage" sections. Not bad, however, the position of the toilet bowls is all wrong—the toilets are facing the door, allowing all the positive energy inside to get flushed away. This may account for why I'm having difficulty using ovulation sticks to determine my LH surge. As a remedy, the book says I absolutely need to keep the lid down at all times.

In addition, both bathrooms are next to each other. This could be confusing the energy or mean I'm destined to have twins! That would be the biggest joke if, after all this, I have twins. I feel awful even admitting this, in light of the extreme difficulty I'm having conceiving, but I'm afraid of having twins. And twins are a distinct possibility when you use fertility drugs. I've seen women in my building struggle with that double stroller. They can't even get into the elevator. And how would I strap on two baby snugglies if I wanted to subway it down to Chelsea to check out an art gallery?

Never mind. I'll take anything.

To enhance the *chi* for fertility, I need to place a photo of a child—or something that I loved as a child—in the bathrooms. Bubble bath counts, even though Mr. Bubble wasn't really allowed in my house because my mother had me convinced I'd get vaginal infections from "that junk they use to make it foam." Even though her claim was baseless, I've graduated to high-end bath products now. I put my favorite foaming lavender bath crystals right on the edge of the tub. At the moment, it's the most childlike thing I can find. I promise myself to search my apartment for one of the Christmas cards our friends sent us with their children lying in a pumpkin patch or sitting on Santa's lap. I never quite know what to do with those photo cards after the holiday season. Throwing them away feels like you're injuring the child somehow. But how long do you have to look at those faces, especially when you're a bit twisted about trying to have a child of your own?

The book says the color white is good for areas designated for creativity and children. So is metal. My bathrooms are all white so I'm good to go there. And the faucets are metal. Another plus. But I needed more! I placed some crystals in the window and considered hanging chimes. Wait! Be subtle. I hate going into people's homes that look like a shrine to mother earth. It looks like they're begging for good luck and serenity. I don't want it to be too obvious to others that I'm wishing for a child. On the other hand, what's wrong with that?

False Hope

I'm late—two days. But late is late. And for someone who checks her nipples on an hourly basis, two days is an eternity. I'm exhausted, which can definitely disrupt any natural flow from my body. I haven't slept in days. Insomnia usually signals the onset of my period. It's like there's a person in my head who refuses to call it a day.

Jewish mysticism teaches that there's a place we go to after we die before we enter heaven. It is in this place that the soul has a chance to make resolution for our less-than-perfect acts in our lives before we can move on to the perfect place. A rabbi I know tells the story that, in this place between dying and heaven, they show two movies—the life you lived and the life you should have lived. All I know is, in these last few months, night after night, the movies about my life are now showing.

I should have gone to overnight camp. I would have developed better separation skills. And why didn't I go away to college? In my neighborhood, not a lot of people left. Our parents gave us the choice of going away to college or getting a car and going to a local college. We all took the cars. Not expensive cars, but something to get us there. I actually thought going away to college was for people who knew what they wanted to do with their lives. I didn't.

"You can be anything you want," my parents insisted. "Just remember we have no money." They loved reminding me, "We are not rich people. If there were only two kinds of people in the world—rich or poor—we'd be considered poor." I knew that we didn't have a lot of money. After all, I had to beg for those Fiorucci jeans. They weren't just handed to me. But poor?

I majored in business. Business meant money. Big mistake. I could feel my soul shutting down the first day of Finance 101 when they showed me the logarithmic curves of investment growth. I persevered. While I struggled with the Keynesian theory of microeconomics, I'm sure all that clenching squeezed my reproductive organs to the point of killing a few dozen eggs.

When I first moved to New York, the first thing my

Trying

Grandmom Ida would ask me when I went to visit her was, "When are you coming back to Philadelphia?"

"I live in New York now," I'd say, trying to exude happiness from every word despite the fact that I was overworked, undersexed and confused about life in general.

"Don't you want to get married?" she'd ask.

"Yes," I'd say. "But right now, I'm working very hard. I work in the garment center. I'm making a good salary. I live on my own. I'll find a husband when I'm ready."

"Oh–h," my grandfather said, his eyes wandering off in thought. "How's your brother? He's a good boy. He has a good job. He makes plenty money. And his wife, Jill, how is she?"

"Fine."

"Do you have a boyfriend?" my grandmother would ask.

"Yes, Grandmom," I said. Sometimes I did and sometimes I didn't.

"I just want to live long enough to see you get married," she'd say. I didn't know what to say to that, so I said, "We'll see."

Every time I left, she'd say the same thing. She'd say, "I just want you to have whatever it is that you want."

Grandmom, you didn't live to see it but I finally got married. He's a nice guy. A very nice guy. But guess what? I may not get everything I want.

Is it morning yet? I've seen enough of this movie.

I got out of bed and hoped my first pee of the day would show some sign of my period coming. I hated to think I lost all this sleep for nothing. Besides, I'd actually been looking forward to getting my period so that I could begin my next round of Fertinex injections. It wasn't coming. And after three days, I went to the store and bought my first pregnancy test—ever.

Mind you, I've never had a lot of close calls. I haven't missed a period since I was 19 and anorexic. The summer after my father's illness, I'd lost 25 pounds and survived on a diet of cantaloupe and carrots. I turned orange. My mother saw how many carrots I devoured on a daily basis and bought me a necklace with a gold charm of a rabbit. A little denial brought to you by the woman who loves you more than anything in the world but is going through her own crisis.

My pregnancy test was negative. What is this, God? Are you delaying my period until *after* the Jewish holidays so I won't have to inject myself on Rosh Hashanah? This is the time of year when Jews around the world celebrate the New Year. It's traditional to tell the story of Hannah and Elkanah. Every day, Hannah went to the temple to pray for a child. She prayed long and hard. Eventually, the praying only came from her heart—her lips moved but no voice was heard. Eli, the high priest, thought she was drunk. But Hannah kept praying and praying until

Trying

God blessed her with a son. I'm worried I don't want a child as much as Hannah did, or that God doesn't think I do. I don't pray as much as she did.

Another matriarch that Jews read about every year during the Jewish High Holidays is Sarah. When she was 90, an angel whispered to her that she was to have a child with Abraham. I'd like to give birth a little sooner than that, preferably before I'm 40.

When I was a little girl, I used to sit on the front steps of my house and count on my fingers all of the older members of my family. There was my Grandmom Belle and my Grandpop Harry. They made two. My Grandpop Abe and Grandmom Ida; that made four. And then there were my parents. All together—six. Six people would have to die before I would ever have to think about dying. When my child worries about dying, he won't be blessed with so many to count. I'd like to be around a while for him or her. I need to hurry.

Next Chapter

I've started taking my video camera with me to my doctor's appointments. I need to have something between the doctor, the stirrups and me. So, during my exams, I rest my camera on my stomach and shoot between my thighs.

My doctor was amazed and slightly put off when I asked him if it would be O.K. if I filmed my examination.

"Are you trying to make a baby or a film?" he asked.

I raised the camera up from between my legs to focus on him as he, now self-consciously, continued the exam. While still looking through the lens, I answered, "Both."

I needed to do something with myself. According to my brother and several other confused family members,

I don't have a real job. Making art—making things—is how I live my life. And yet, I was hesitant about making a video. I wanted to separate the girl who used to make raw, performance art videos from the woman who is now older, married and trying to have a baby. Until now.

During my trips to the doctor, I'd often watch some of the women in the waiting room pull out their cell phones from their briefcases and begin making calls. I'd listen as they speak to their assistants giving them a "to do" list and confirm the day's appointments. Eavesdropping on self-important, overachieving women is nauseating enough. But then I'd hear them checking in with their nannies and ask to speak to their child.

"Mommy will be home later tonight. Kiss. Kiss," they'd say while looking for a pen in their purse.

I hate people who use the phrase "kiss kiss." I get the feeling that even if they were standing directly in front of you, they'd avoid actually kissing you in favor of saying those words.

It wasn't that long ago that I was still making videos. In fact, two of my works were currently on exhibition as part of a group show traveling across the country. Several months ago, the show was in my hometown of Philadelphia. When I first heard the show was coming, I dreamed of arriving at the opening dressed in postpartum chic—a flowing, black tunic over cigarette leg pants, and cuddling a baby in my arms. Instead, I carried a round of fertility drugs and a 50cc syringe in my purse.

Trying

Round Two

The time it takes for me to prepare the drug and puncture my thigh has improved. At night, I do the whole thing between the 11:20 weather report and *Nightline* at 11:30. It feels great to be doing something again. I've waited two months since my last round of Fertinex because my doctor told me that my ovaries needed down time. I don't blame them. The month I stimulated, I could feel my ovaries whenever I walked. Pockets of stimulated follicles bounced around in me like ping pong balls, only heavier; jostling around my pelvis trying to find a place for themselves.

The nurse in charge of scheduling told me that the soonest I'd be able to have an in vitro fertilization would be sometime in January, which means we have time for at least one more round of stimulation in the hopes of avoiding IVF all together. Before starting, my doctor took another blood test to check my FSH. If my level is too high, it indicates that my hormones are already working overtime and this wouldn't be a good month to stimulate. FSH levels can fluctuate from month to month, but each time I get a high reading, it means there are fewer and fewer good eggs left. That number is a reminder that my biological clock is ticking.

Throughout my single years, I never felt rushed by time, just nudged a little. I also wasn't aware that I was suffering from "diminished ovarian reserve." If I knew I was officially running out of eggs, I wouldn't have been so casual about baby-making. The moment Oliver and I realized we were going to spend the rest of our lives together, we should have started to try. Instead, I wanted to look thin in my wedding dress—the slim one with the halter back and fine Italian lace that my saleslady said, "Could only be worn by a person with your body."

The day I walked into the bridal department of Bergdorf Goodman, I was wearing black jeans and motorcycle boots. I was ignored. As I helped myself through racks filled with imported satin and lace, I heard a "May I help you?" from a large, blond woman rising from her seat behind a French Provincial desk. I told her I was getting married in June.

"How lovely!" she said. "May I see your ring?" (which is code for, "How much can you spend on a dress?")

The joke was on her. I'd never pay retail! I know too many people in the business. This was purely research. She led me into the bridal dressing room where I put on the dress that inspired a vision of me slipping in and out of the arms of friends while table-hopping at the Boathouse in Central Park. I called my friend Cliff from a phone conveniently installed inside the dressing room and asked him if he could come over to see the dress *immediately*. Cliff designs women's eveningwear and generously offered his talent in searching for the perfect dress, and then knocking it off.

Trying

My mother went to the Blue Bird Bridal Shop for *her* wedding dress. My Aunt Lil, my father's sister, worked there. Aunt Lil smoked Parliament cigarettes, which she kept in a metallic gold case with a matching lighter. She wore a ring that said "Love" on one side and "Fuck" on the other. Despite my mother's less-than-thrilled opinion of her, I loved my Aunt Lil. She was the person in my life who convinced my mother I was old enough to wear lip-gloss, and gave me my first tube of mascara, which she slipped to me after one of my excursions into her handbag.

The day my mother went to buy a wedding dress, my aunt took measurements of my mother's bust and told the other salesgirls, "My brother's getting gypped."

For years, my mother's wedding dress sat in my closet in a bag. I'd always been too scared to look at it. Then one day, after I was engaged and Oliver was over, I took a deep breath, pulled the dress down from the closet, threw it over my head, opened my eyes and exhaled. It was nicer than I remembered, especially now that I'd tried on a few. I imagined Flossie, as her maid of honor, helping my mother with the rows of satin-covered buttons on the sleeves. Before allowing myself to feel sad, I walked over to Oliver who helped me button up the back as far as it would go. I looked in the mirror. It fit—sort of. I was thinner than my mother. But even if it fit perfectly, my heart told me that I didn't want to bring this ghost to my wedding. As it is, many of the guests will probably be in tears as I walk down the aisle without my parents. Besides, my mother would want me to have a new dress.

Every week, I returned to Seventh Avenue to watch my wedding dress being made. Anita, the head seamstress in Cliff's office, was from Croatia and knew everything about working with Italian lace. "Only for you, Barbara," she yelled, as she measured the fabric over and over to be sure the edge of each flower lined up exactly with the other. As she worked, Anita told me stories about her years with some of the big fashion houses. "I once made a dress for Mamie Eisenhower," she said. "It was 1956 and, I assure you, I was *much* younger than Mamie. Mamie was a size 12—an alcoholic, but a nice size 12!"

My Grandmom Ida made dresses "for all the fancy ladies" when she lived in Russia. In this country, she worked in a grocery store that she ran with my grandfather. I remember sitting in her kitchen drinking tea while sucking on a cube of sugar, with pictures of Golda Meir and Moshe Dayan looking down at us. My mother would often send me with a bag of clothes for my grandmother to mend. I loved sitting alongside her watching her hands work the needle and thread as she went over and over the same spot until the hole disappeared.

The women making my wedding dress used old-fashioned Singer sewing machines just like the ones my grandmothers had—the kind that were operated by foot pedals. I'd stand for as long as the seamstress would let me, watching her foot rock back and forth, back and forth, as all the pieces came together.

The day my dress was finished, everyone who worked on it came into the back room as I carefully stepped into the transformed layers of silk, satin and lace. Anita proudly fastened my train, then took a few steps back to examine her work. As she reached over to snip off a stray thread, she hugged me and started to cry. I cried, too, for all the women who never got to see me in my dress.

Without Warning

At the beginning of my recent acupuncture session, I rested my hands in the therapist's as she felt my pulse.

"Have you been crying?" she asked.

"Not really," I said. I wasn't going to tell her that I'd spent the past two days reading through my old journals—boxes of them—searching for evidence of the life I'd been living all those years while not becoming a mother.

"Did anything happen today to upset you?"

"Maybe." That day, I learned about Robin. Robin and I work out together at the gym and, over the last few months, we'd become friends. She's a year older than me, a painter, and shared my concern about pursuing her art while trying to start a family. She and her husband were trying, as she put it, "a little." She also knew that Oliver and I had been trying "more than a little." At the gym, a place where I valued my privacy, she was an insider. She knew about all my tests and my recent surgery.

That morning, we were on the exercise bikes talking about local restaurants, movies, her new piece. And then, "Look at these!" she says, pointing to her bouncing chest. "I'm pregnant."

I was stunned. Not that she was pregnant, but that she didn't give me any warning. She didn't try to tell me her great news with any sensitivity for how it might make me feel. And then she says, "I was thinking about you s–o–o much when I found out."

Oh, O.K. *Now* she realizes she might have been too blunt. Then she says, "I thought about you so much because you and I, we both don't have our mothers!"

Oh my God! Is she for real? To avoid further depression, I did what I usually do in the spirit of overcompensation: I volunteered to take her to lunch.

That night, Oliver sat down to Chinese food and *Seinfeld* reruns and I say, "Guess what? Robin's pregnant."

"What? Jesus!" he yelled. "Did you have to tell me that way, without any warning?"

"Well I didn't think you'd react like that," I said. "*I'm* not surprised. I mean, I . . . we both knew they were trying."

"Is that how she told *you*?" he asked.

I told Oliver what happened at the gym.

"But did you have to come out and tell *me* like that? Couldn't you have been a little gentler? Like, 'Oliver, I have some news about one of my friends. It's good, but it was hard for me to hear.'" He kept going. "You are so mean! WHAT IS WRONG WITH YOU?"

"I'm sorry. I mean, you're right. I could have, I should have!" I blurted out. "I guess I wanted you to feel what I felt when she told me."

"You succeeded."

The next day, I assume the womb harmony pose in the sunlight of my living room and meditate on the child that wants to come down from the heavens and join me. Is there a child up there? I can't see! I've been on drugs for five days. In another day, it will be time for my shot of HCG, the drug that induces ovulation. Then I will go in for the insemination. I have to believe one of these eggs is carrying the soul that's meant for Oliver and me to care for.

As I lay on the floor, I wondered about the people who get pregnant right away. What do they obsess about, if anything? The color of their baby's room? Names? Breast or bottle? They're lucky. Right now, I'm obsessing about sex. I'm tired of it. Friends warned us not to start trying right away. I thought they were trying to tell me that the stress of raising a newborn isn't healthy so soon in a marriage. But now, I realize that it's the trying that will kill your sex life. Lately, even when we're not trying, when we're simply making love, I monitor every move. Has Oliver always kissed this way? Why doesn't my head know which way to tilt? His arm feels too heavy on my stomach. Someone once said this about making love: if you have to stop and ask yourself if you're having a good time, then you're not.

When Oliver and I were first dating and the sex was good, I was excited by the prospect of spending the rest of my life with someone who could make me feel that good. So good that it made me want to be better in bed. When I went to visit my friend Jeptha, who was recently separated, we went to a bookstore and bought all the latest how-to books and gave ourselves a refresher course in sex. Sitting on her sofa while her two-year-old daughter slept in the other room, we read each other tips on fellatio.

I always felt my sexiest when my relationships weren't serious. Those were the days when I went to bed without wearing a shirt and I stayed that way till morning (although I might have worn socks). I had that feeling that made me want to make love the minute they walked in the door. Or in the middle of the night. Or first thing in the morning. I was willing to try almost anything, too, especially if the guy I was sleeping with lived in another state or another country.

When Oliver and I got serious, I panicked. I looked for a way out. The first thing I decided after spending a few nights in his apartment was that he must be gay. I couldn't understand how a straight man could have a wall filled with Stephen Sondheim posters and another that featured a *Torch Song Trilogy* poster above his grand piano. It looked just like the sing-a-long bars I'd visited in the Village with my gay buddies. Also, the man's shoes were all lined up in a drawer under his bed, complete with shoe trees. I confronted him. "It's O.K. if you are, just tell me. I can handle it." Turns out, the man just liked theater, and he was tired of piling his shoes on top of each other.

Next, I decided Oliver must be taking antidepressants. When I met him, he was barely making ends meet as a free-lance journalist. He was in the process of selling his co-op apartment at a loss to avoid bankruptcy, and yet he sounded so chipper every time he called me for a date. "Hey Barb. It's me, Oliver. How'd you like to take our bikes out and go for a ride?" Oliver used to be a disc jockey and has the kind of voice that has an annoyingly positive inflection. He was financially distressed and vocationally unstable. Who the hell is this happy unless they're taking drugs? And that could explain why he sweated excessively every time he drank a glass of water. Enough. I'd been through too much in my life to get involved with someone, only to find out they have a chemical dependency. Besides, I'd already dated that.

I called Oliver. "I really need to talk to you. Could you please come over?" He said yes. Amazing! Every man I'd ever known would have said, "What? Tell me now!"

if I had asked them to come over. Not Oliver—he's very patient. He's also not Jewish. No Jew would wait for you to tell them something in person.

When he came over, I said, "You seem to be so happy all the time. And sometimes I notice that your hands shake and you've been sweating a lot. I recounted all the symptoms I'd learned from a friend whose boyfriend was on Prozac. For the second time in two weeks, I heard myself say, "Don't be afraid to tell me. I just want to know."

"First of all, I'm not taking antidepressants," he said, gently explaining that his hands shake sometimes from taking antihistamines and that he usually sweats whenever he drinks cold water quickly. "But, Barb, even if I *was* taking anti-depressants," he added, "you shouldn't stigmatize people who have chemical imbalances."

Oliver was right. In fact, there are days I think my bravado—my philosophy of "just saying no" to Valium or Prozac or whatever pharmaceutical substance was offered to me by my therapists over the years, was not such a good thing. Drugs might have helped. All those sleepless nights, all those years of walking around exhausted and strung out on coffee. I may have destroyed my eggs.

My demons have returned. I know them well and they are magnified by my infertility. They dress up like desire and make me long for the guy I dated right before Oliver. The one I didn't stay with because I decided he wasn't the relationship type and I wanted something real.

Trying

I long for him. I long for just about anybody other than Oliver.

There are days I wonder if I'm having sex with Oliver because I want to make love or because I want to make a baby. Am I tired of having sex because I'm tired of sex with Oliver, or because we did it six times in five days?

When Oliver and I are *not* trying to make a baby, we have license to do anything we want—any position, any time, unlimited orgasms. But somehow, "doing it" on the kitchen floor is no longer an exciting alternative. These days, doing nothing is.

Oliver's been looking for a new job, which means he's been home a lot. *Too* much. It's great when I have a doctor's appointment and he comes with me. Or when we have lunch at our local diner and talk. It's great—two people at home all the time, sharing thoughts and feelings. But this isn't normal. Shouldn't one of us be racing out of the house to an office complaining that we never get to see each other? Then, when I get pregnant, I could spend my time worrying whether or not Oliver will be home at a normal hour for dinner, followed by quality time with our child. I already know he would. But what if he doesn't find another job? What if he slips into a depression and spends his days playing solitaire on our computer? Then we'll have nothing but a depressed, childless home. I'm tired of trying.

Oliver will give me my HCG shot tonight. This is the BIG needle. Unlike last time, I'm planning to watch the home improvement channel. I think it will be helpful for me to focus on something else, like how to resurface an antique wooden chair. As Oliver prepares the needles, I can lose myself in the rhythm of sanding and then applying that first thin coat of non-latex primer. The next thing I know, the shot will be over.

Tomorrow is the insemination. I mark my calendar so I know when to expect or, hopefully, *not* get my period. Twenty-four years ago today was my Bat Mitzvah. I was 13 and standing in Shaare Shamayim synagogue in front of a room full of people reciting my *Haftorah* and making my parents proud. I wonder if I'm infertile because I married somebody who isn't Jewish. Am I supposed to get divorced so that I'll be able to conceive with some guy named Goldberg? I start to panic. I need to think. If I don't get pregnant this month and Oliver doesn't get a job, maybe it's a sign. I should leave him.

Leave him? To go where? It's Oliver who keeps me sane. The other night, I asked him to tell me how *he* was feeling. I don't want to corner the market on emotional upheaval.

"Are you sad you married me?" I asked. "Aren't you angry? Don't you ever think that if this doesn't work out, you'd want a whole other life?" I'm aware that in our relationship, I assume the role of the drama queen. But I figure if I say the unthinkable, Oliver won't feel so bad about admitting that the thought occurred to him, too. Only it hasn't.

Trying

"How can you say these things?" he asked me.

"Well you always tell me stories about how, when you were five, you gave rides in your little red wagon to all the girls in the neighborhood and sketched out your dream house—including children—when you were six. I don't even remember playing house. If it was supposed to happen, it would have. And because it didn't, maybe . . ."

"Stop!" Oliver said. I pause and listen, praying something he says will make it all go away. "I want a life with you. If we have a baby, so much the better. But if we don't, I still have you and I'm grateful for that."

He is so sure. I'm not. I planned on a *family* right about now. And if it's not happening, I'm thinking that a pueblo in Santa Fe where I'd paint pictures of empty wombs might be in my future.

Maybe infertility is God's way of telling me I'm not supposed to be married at all. I should have many lovers, many experiences, live alone to pursue some important work I haven't thought of yet. In the biblical story of Hannah and Elkanah, Elkanah couldn't understand why Hannah was so miserable after 10 years of a happy, yet childless marriage. Elkanah said to her, "Why do you weep? Am I not better to you than 10 sons?" She didn't answer.

Is it possible that I married Oliver only to have children? I rerun our last few years together looking for a sign that I might have been deluding myself. I never lived with anyone before Oliver. When we decided to move in together, we both left our old apartments behind to look for a new beginning together. I moved from my Mary Tyler Moore studio apartment into a classic six with river views. It was more than we wanted to spend on rent, but it was the West Side apartment both of us dreamed of after years of watching Woody Allen movies. We pictured ourselves entertaining our friends in a real dining room, spreading the Sunday Times all over the living room floor and still having room for bagels, and watching the boats go by while we got dressed in the morning. Yet despite the extra room, I felt cramped hearing both of our names on one answering machine. I remember the pangs I felt when it occurred to me that any guy I ever knew who might call me on a whim will know I'm committed. I never realized what it was like to go home to the same person every day of your life. I hadn't had a roommate of any kind since I was 23.

Living together wasn't all bad. I remember walking up Broadway getting excited that I would see Oliver when I got home. I always had so much I wanted to tell him. Every day he made me laugh. And every night would end with me lying on his chest, watching 11:30 reruns of Frasier.

Then Oliver gave me the best present of my life. He gave me a story. One morning at 7am, just three weeks after moving in together and days before my thirty-fifth birthday, Oliver woke me up and said, "Every day in life has the possibility of being an exceptional day, and today is an exceptional day."

"Uh-huh," I mumbled. "Nice try." I didn't want to get out of bed. I had to meet with my graduate school advisors that day to hear them critique my plans for my final video exhibition. It was so like Oliver to give me a little pep talk.

"No really," he said, nodding his head. "Today is an exceptional day. In five hours, a car is picking us up. We're flying to Paris."

"We are not!" I screeched.

"We're going," Oliver said laughing at me and grabbing his briefcase from next to our bed. "Here, look! These are the tickets."

"Is this a joke? If this is a joke, I swear to God." I was afraid to let my excitement register.

When he pulled out the guidebooks to Paris and Florence, I believed him. We were doing something I'd only fantasized about—leaving for Europe on a moment's notice. One night in Florence as we walked past the Ponte Vecchio toward our hotel, Oliver suggested we walk up to the rooftop terrace. Overlooking the city, I told him, "If we're going to be together, you can't just do nice things for me. You have to remember to do nice things for yourself."

"O.K., I will," he said. And he got down on one knee and asked me to marry him.

To hear Oliver tell this, my first words were, "Get the

hell outta here!" which is true. But after that I said, "I'd love to." I knew I'd wanted to marry Oliver ever since we sat in Maine exchanging stories of our childhood. I even promised myself that if he proposed, I'd say yes immediately. I loved him, but I knew that my fears have a way of preventing me from being in my own life.

Back then, I was scared of committing to someone because I knew marriage was about sharing a lifetime of experiences—and not just the good ones. At the time, Oliver still had his father, but I was already picturing what it would be like when he died. I thought about Oliver and I growing old together and all the debilitating illnesses that might plague us. Staring up at the moon that night in Florence, I even flashed on the funerals we would attend together. I never considered infertility.

After my parents died, I lost all normal expectations, like having them around to hear about my career, the men I'd meet, the man I'd marry. I decided the only way to survive was to reinvent myself. I took classes in everything from bookbinding to Buddhism (that was just the B section of the New School catalogue). I read, I wrote, I traveled. I was alone *a lot*. I was after adventure for adventure's sake and became so good at believing I was on the road to finding myself, I didn't notice that I was running from myself.

Now, faced with the possibility that I won't be able to make a child, I try to keep busy, stay positive. But I'm feeling that familiar fear. Once again, someone has their hand on my back and they're pushing me faster than I want to go. I feel like starting my life all over. For the second time this month, I walked into our guest bedroom where Oliver was working at the desk and made an announcement.

"I'm very unhappy," I started. "I don't think I love you enough."

"What?"

"I'm thinking that if we can't have a child, I'm not sure I see us together anymore."

"Not this again. First of all, how do you even know we can't? And besides, we just started trying. What the hell are you talking about?" he said, looking at me scared, confused and angry. "I already told you! I didn't marry you just to have a child. I love YOU. Having a child is a bonus."

That was such a sweet thing to say, it made me feel even worse. Oliver is so good. I am so bad.

"I think that if I really loved you, maybe none of this would be happening."

"You're insane," he said somehow with a half-smile. He sensed my fear.

"Come over here."

"NO."

"Then come over here to say your last goodbyes." He stands up and starts waving his right arm. "Goodbye person who rubs your back no matter how tired he is! Goodbye person who tells you the play-by-play of Frasier episodes you fell asleep to! Goodbye person who brings you a snack in bed every night and un-tucks the blankets at the bottom of the bed to liberate your feet! Goodbye! Goodbye!"

With each goodbye, his arms got wider and wider, trying to make me laugh. I did laugh, but mostly out of nervousness.

I couldn't believe I made Oliver so scared and that he was strong enough to take it. Right now, I think Oliver loves me a lot more than I love myself.

"We have a good life," he reminds me. "We travel, we have great friends, we have each other. If this doesn't work, if we can't have a baby, we can always adopt. And even if we decide not to, we'll still have a good life."

I need to remember that, even though this is happening to *my* body, infertility is OUR problem. Oliver handles the stress of infertility different than I do. We'll kiss each other good night, turn over and go to sleep. The next morning, when we are having breakfast, he hands me a stack of articles he pulled off the web about FSH, in vitro fertilization or premature ovarian failure. In the hours I managed to get some sleep, Oliver was up for hours searching for answers via the internet.

"I'm making Oliver nuts!" I told my friend Birgitta the other day over lunch. Birgitta and I went to art school together and pride ourselves in being masters of self-sabotage.

"I'm not sure I love him enough," I confessed.
"I hope to God you didn't tell him that," she said.
"I did. I had to. That's who we are," I admitted.
"He's so great," she sighed.
"I know. That's what makes me feel even worse."

Right after my parents died, I had a boyfriend break up with me because he told me I needed him too much, which was ironic as I never felt like I got close enough to need anyone. Over the phone he said, "I can be your lover and your friend, but I cannot give you what you lost in your mother and father."

He never met an Oliver.

The morning of my insemination, the doctor handed me the test tube of Oliver's sperm for me to check the label and make sure it was ours. I'm feeling very separate from Oliver. The first time I was inseminated was novel; there was something slightly romantic in the mystery of it all. This time, it was routine and depressing. I felt totally disconnected from our goal. Other people had warned me that fertility treatments "couldn't be more mechanical." I hadn't gotten to that point. Now, I had.

Instead of relaxing on the table visualizing Oliver's sperm swimming upstream to my eggs, I found myself wondering if I still wanted a child . . . enough. Maybe I'm so caught up in the frenzy of infertility treatments that I've lost sight of what my infertility might be trying to tell me. Maybe I'm supposed to go through this life alone. It's so like me to reject the joyful possibility that I just might get pregnant this time. Happiness terrifies me.

The Wait

The last few days, I've been on jury duty. Today, during the voir dire process, the bailiff caught me checking my breasts. The lawyers don't want you to read or write or do anything that might be distracting. They just want you to sit back and listen, which I did, until I found myself sliding my hand under my shirt to check for nipple tenderness. Every time I got moved from one courtroom to the next, my hand found its way inside my coat, under my sweater, then into my camisole. I've stopped wearing bras. They made me too conscious of minor fluctuations in breast size. I am a week away from my period. There's still time for a miracle.

I went to see my acupuncturist for a relaxation treatment. I looked into her eyes while she checked my pulse and examined the quadrants of my tongue. Am I pregnant? Maybe she knows, but won't say. I would not let myself be fooled by swollen breasts. In fact, I was bracing myself for the fall.

I know the ritual. First, I see the thread of pink on the toilet tissue. Then I tell myself that some people stain when they're pregnant. The whole day I try not to pee, praying that my period has not really come. When I can't wait another minute, I go to the bathroom and see a drop of crimson in the toilet bowl, then a teaspoon, then enough to warrant a tampon. That's when the illusion ends—when I can no longer deny reality and I turn my thoughts to the next month. And the countdown begins: 11 more days until ovulation.

My acupuncturist told me about an herbal supplement that she says lowers FSH levels. I've been trying to time the taking of this supplement, which can only be taken for six weeks at a time, to when they'll re-test me to determine whether I'm still eligible for in vitro fertilization. If my FSH level is lower than 10, they will proceed with IVF. If my level is *over* 10, I'm out of their program. No second chances.

During my last sonogram, I told my doctor I was considering taking Chinese herbs. I could see his hesitation, so I said it first.

"I know it won't change the *quality* of my eggs, just my FSH level," I told him, trying to sound like I understood my fate even though I wasn't ready to accept it.

"As long as you know," he said.

The herbs needed to be mixed with warm water and taken three times a day. If you've ever had your floors sanded and have lived amidst the wood dust that settles everywhere, that's the consistency. The solution is absolutely like taking that dust, adding water, and swallowing it. It smells like the paneling that was in my family room in the 70s.

The acupuncturist also gave me a green bottle of

herbs to help me sleep because I keep waking up in the middle of the night. It's not that I've lost all hope, but that heart-beating excitement of imagining a new person forming in my body—that feeling I had when we first starting trying—isn't there anymore. It hurts too much when I'm wrong.

Last night, I dreamt I was being inseminated, though not with sperm. In my dream, the doctors are trying to insert a small baby, three or four months old, inside my uterus. I have to lie under water while a nurse leads the child into my vagina to see if it will swim up. After trying several times, the baby is getting closer to entering my body, but doesn't. That was when the nurse showed me the baby's eyes.

"Don't show me!" I yelled, catching a glimpse of his soul. "In case it doesn't work."

It was a long process, trying to make the baby go in. The water level kept getting higher and higher around my head. Soon, I was under water along with my child. I couldn't breathe. I had to stop them. I pulled my head out of the water.

"Wait!" I said. "I need a break."

"But the baby," they said. "It needs to go in!"

I slowly caught my breath, and while the baby waited to go in, I woke up. I'm going to be very, very nice to myself today.

I saw the pale pink hue on the toilet tissue even earlier

than the doctor had warned. I was only on Day 22. The next day my period was quite heavy. I wondered if it was the result of all my unused eggs. That night at dinner, a friend asked me where I was in "the process." She's nice enough to call it *that*, now. I didn't have the strength to tell her the insemination failed. I simply said, "Waiting to see."

The Ladies Who Lunch

My friend Mary and two of her closest women friends are coming to New York for our annual Christmas lunch. In the latest impossible-to-get-a-reservation-at-night-but-perfect-for-a-decadent-lunch restaurant, we drink champagne and applaud each other's accomplishments: a new home, a better job, a new baby. This year, I consider it an accomplishment that I'm even going to this lunch.

Mary and I used to work as sales representatives for several women's clothing companies. I was 23 and, besides a brief stint working as a producer for a call-in talk show where I got fired for letting too many devil worshippers get through to the host (it wasn't my fault the caller from Ardmore, PA didn't profess his satanic ways until he got on the air), it was my first real job. As a sales rep, I'd get into my car every morning and travel to one of five states surrounding Philadelphia lugging a rolling clothing rack filled with garment bags. At the time, I still lived with my parents and I loved waking up and driving to a different city. My mother wasn't as thrilled by the job.

"Can't you sell nicer clothes?" my mother once asked me upon examining the clothes I'd stored in our den. Admittedly, drop-waisted, polyester-printed dresses didn't have the greatest appeal, but I loved trying to get people to buy them.

"Can't you teach smarter children?" I snapped back.

She never seemed to mind when I sent her a designer dress for wholesale or, even better, for free. Then it was, "Look what my Barbie got for me!"

My father didn't love my job either. I'd call him at 10 o'clock at night from a town outside of Baltimore because my car was making a funny, clicking noise.

"Don't you belong to Three As?" he'd ask me, in a voice half-asleep.

"Yes."

"So, call them," he'd say. Truth is, even after I called them, my dad would usually drive to wherever I was and bring me home.

Mary loves reminding me of the day I walked confidently into the office of Simon's Millinery Mart ready to begin my career in sales. I was fresh out of college with a degree in marketing. She was a graduate of the school of hard knocks. I wore black slacks, a crème-colored blouse and, I'm sad to say, a vest. Mary sat at her desk wearing beat-up jeans. As she watched me peruse some blank order forms while I waited to see my new boss, I caught her rolling her eyes.

The first day Mary took me out for training as a "roadie," she couldn't believe just how clueless I was. When I stopped at the entrance to the turnpike, I didn't know how to remove the ticket. When she handed me the map and told me to find the exit number for Allentown, I simply told her, "I can't read maps." And when we arrived at our first account, I apparently stood idly by and watched in amazement as she assembled the rolling rack by herself and heaved several large bags of clothing the size of body bags up onto the bar. Is it my fault that, up until then, my idea of long-distance driving was the hour I commuted from my house in the suburbs to Temple University in Center City, Philadelphia? I thought four years of commuting qualified as a lot of driving experience.

However, as much as Mary loves to tell everyone how naïve I was, I like to think I taught her a few things about being a professional. Before I came along, Mary was the type of person who'd get up at four in the morning to drive hours to get to a department store in D.C. by nine. But I explained to her that, if it took four hours to drive to a particular store, then you need to make the appointment for sometime around noon. After a few appointments in the same area, an overnight stay is required because I don't believe in driving home through the night. And if an overnight stay is required, we should never sleep on the outskirts of town in motels that are suggested by our boss. You know, the ones that offer nothing more than a bible and a stack of hangers in case we run into trouble. For the money we made for our boss, let's just see if they have a suite at that Hyatt I noticed on our way into town.

I remember the day my mother came downtown to my office and announced to my boss, "Hello everyone. I've come to take my princess out to lunch." Mary looked horrified. I did too, but I went and took Mary with us.

After my first grueling month in New York working like a slave on Seventh Avenue, Mary showed up at my apartment with champagne, a homemade apple pie from her mom, and a large bottle of vitamins. We have always been there to fortify each other, but lately, infertility seems to be a dividing line. She's busy moving forward with her life while mine seems to be standing still.

This year's lunch at Mercer Kitchen marks my fourteenth year in New York City. By now, all the women at the table except me have become mothers. They know that Oliver and I have been trying since our last Christmas get-together when I was afraid to drink any champagne. I'm drinking today. I don't care. Besides, these women are full of stories about how they did *everything* and still got pregnant.

"I know this sounds crazy," one of the women insisted

on telling me. "But, my doctor told me to drink cough syrup. And I don't know how, but it worked!"

"Great!" I said. "I'm going to the bathroom." I needed to rejuvenate for the round of pictures and storytelling that would accompany dessert. Do I sound bitter? On the contrary, I've been exemplary at setting aside my problems while joining others to celebrate their families. The women tell me about the lunch date they just had with their mother, or the weekends their mother comes over to watch the kids, or how their parents "just love taking Matthew on the train" or "Samantha to see the *Nutcracker*."

I also hear about the grandparents who aren't as eager to give up their weekends to baby-sit because they have new husbands or a house in Florida or are too busy traveling. And when the grandparents *are* around, my friends tell me that they can't stand it when their mother insists on telling them what to do. I don't think my mother would be like that.

My mother prefaced any sentence that she knew might lead to confrontation with, "Am I allowed to know?" as in, "Am I allowed to know why you have your sofa on that side of the room?" Other times she would remove herself entirely from the line of fire by saying to me, "Can a person ask a question?"

I loved telling my mother about my life, but she was right when she told me I didn't leave myself open for comments. She would say, "You tell me that you want to tell me something but that I can *not* offer an opinion. So I listen to you. Then you ask me what I think and I tell you. And then you tell me to mind my own business!"

I miss that.

A few years after my mother died, I told my friend Gary that I hated my mother. Gary, who'd known me since college said, "You don't hate your mother. You just don't have the guts to miss her."

He was right.

I told the women around our Christmas luncheon that I, too, felt in conflict with my mother. "YOU?" they asked in disbelief. "Isn't your mother . . . ?"

"Yes, she is," I told them. "But I consider these problems dead or alive issues. Just because she's dead doesn't mean that I've separated from her."

Is it Sometimes yet?

On the way home from lunch, I wondered if I've prayed hard enough to my mother to help me get a child. Have I prayed to her at all? Have I directly asked her to help me get a child? No. I've prided myself in leaving her out of this. Maybe she's insulted. Mom? Mom! I'm having major fertility issues. It's been 10 years since I broke up with Jonathan. Is it sometimes yet?

A year ago, a woman who worked with Oliver had lost her father. The week he died, she spent the afternoon with a psychic that, she insisted, communicated with her deceased father. The psychic recalled how he died, what he was wearing when they buried him, and generally—no, *specifically*—how he was doing.

In all the years since my parent's death, I had never gone to a psychic—at least not one who claims to speak directly with the deceased. I *had* attempted to meditate with my guardian angels, performed various candlelighting ceremonies and crystallized all of my chakras. But I'd never actually tried to talk with my mother through another person. Partly because I believed I knew as much as any psychic does, and partly from fear. If this person was truly able to conduct a conversation between my mother and me, I wasn't ready. But during the week of my thirty-sixth birthday, I decided I wanted to do something special. I couldn't resist a chance to have lunch with my mother.

Nancy B. sat in the corner of the room in a big club chair with an ottoman, while I sat 10 feet away on a long sofa with a coffee table in front. I felt uncomfortable having this much furniture between us. I'd imagined us hovered over a dimly-lit table with a crystal ball, maybe a candle or a cup of tea. I'd even brought along pictures of my mother and pieces of her jewelry to help with the vibrations. No such objects were requested.

She began our session by chatting about the traffic down the West Side Highway and telling me something about the guy who she saw before me. I don't remember what she said because I was only listening for these words: "Barbara, who would you like me to contact?"

Instead, her first question was, "How's your husband?" Huh?

"It's seems there is dysfunction within his family," she went on.

"Not really," I said.

"Work then. Something at work," she probed. "Is he having trouble at work?"

"Yes," I nodded.

"He needs to look elsewhere," she says. "Has he been looking to change his job? He should."

Why are we talking about *him*? I want my mother.

"His father," she continued, pointing to her chest. "I'm seeing something here. The man had heart surgery, did he not?" she said. "Yes, he did." I told her, building up some confidence in this psychic.

"Tell him he shouldn't be afraid of slowing down."

"O.K., I'll tell him," I said.

"And his mother," she continued. "Did she cut her hand?"

"No." I said, getting impatient. I'm not even *telling* her that his mother's been dead for 12 years. We're here to talk about *my* mother. I kept trying to refocus my energy on my mother. Mom, Mom, Mom. Come in, Mommy. I'm over here in this living room.

"I see you experienced a great loss 10 years ago," she says.

Trying

O.K.! Now we're talking.

"You're fine, now," she said, looking at me like a mother who checks her child's temperature before sending him back to school.

"Is your father alive?" she asked.

"You want *me* to tell *you*?" I asked this nationally acclaimed, widely published, highly-paid psychic.

I desperately wanted her to locate my mother, so I offered the circumstances of her death so we could get down to it already.

"They died together." I said. "In a fire." There. That should speed things up.

"It wasn't their fault," she said. It wasn't in their house."

"No, it wasn't." I said, vowing to offer no more details.

She shifted in her chair, silent for the moment, head tilted, looking into the air as if to see beyond the fireplace beside her. Perhaps my mother's spirit was present!

"Boy that was rough!" she says, clutching her heart. "Ouch! But . . . you're fine now! A ball of energy. You are doing great! You married a rational man. You're very together. Now, does your husband know anyone whose name starts with the letter "D." I keep seeing it very clearly—"D."

She sees "D" and she doesn't see my mother?

"Maybe," I said, refusing to elaborate. Apparently, my husband's job search was eating into her psyche as well as the time I'm supposed to be having with my mother. But what if this lady has a job lead? I'd better listen.

"I see him out of there by January. Definitely. Out. Tell him to start looking," she insisted.

Finally, seeing she wasn't picking up on any of *my* needs, I said, "I want to know about my mother."

"Have you mourned?" she asked.

"Of course I've mourned!" I told her. "I've done it all," I said, without divulging my seven years on the couch, my work in art therapy and my religious devotion. "I'd just like to check in with her. It's been 10 years since her death. In many ways, my life has never been better. How is my mother doing? How does she think *I'm* doing?"

"She's not here," she snaps, adjusting her shirtsleeves. "She's part of the universe already. Read my book. You'll understand." I read her book. It talked all about energy and loved ones and the vibrations from their spirit whenever they choose to surround you. Vibrations are nice, but my friend *heard* her father. I want to hear my mother—*now*.

"Does your husband need to stay in journalism?" she asks. "I see him in other areas—historic novels, for example."

"O.K.," I said, after we successfully mapped out my husband's career path with people whose names start with the letter "D." If the dead are transformed into energy, how come other people get to *see* the dead? My friend Jaimee saw her Grandma Fanny in the medicine cabinet. Her husband, Michael, saw his friend Al standing by the side of his bed in a sports jacket and sneakers. I'm as spiritual as the next person—more spiritual. I've seen *nothing*."

I didn't tell her about the nights I go into my kitchen and concentrate, *O.K., Mom, I'm here. Come on in. Please!! Break open the Pepperidge Farm Milanos I've been saving for just this occasion and we'll talk.* Then I get terrified. Before I even turn on the light, I start to think that if she's actually standing in my kitchen I will absolutely have a heart attack. So it's probably better that she doesn't appear.

"It's not in your Karma to be a clairvoyant in this life," the psychic says.

Was she telling me I was not good enough to see my mother?

"You'll see her when you pass over," she said. "But that's a long time from now, a very long time."

Well that's certainly nice to hear. But this session was costing me $175.00 an hour. My mother would kill me if she knew I was spending this kind of money, but apparently she has no idea I'm even sitting in this room. She only feels vibrations.

"Listen," she said. "You need to listen more." Oh, now *that* sounds like my mother.

She told me how my mother did come to me in thoughts and in dreams, which I already knew. That wasn't enough. I wanted more.

"I need confirmation," I told her. "I need to know."

"If she was at your wedding?" she asked.

"Yes."

"It doesn't work that way," she told me. "She isn't in one place then another."

She paused, her gaze returning to the air. Mom? Is that my mom?

"I see you molding something with your hands. Do you work in clay?"

"Never."

"Photographs. I see you surrounded by lots of images." That's true. Lucky guess.

She wanted to talk about what I'm into now. "The now is fine," I told her. "I got married four months ago. I was recently in my first big art exhibition. I just received my master's degree. My husband and I are very much in love and have just started trying to have a baby. Can I speak to my mother *now*?"

"You have beautiful clothes," she said. My mistake. I looked too good for someone in need of a talk with her mother. Next time I go to a psychic, I'm going in ripped jeans.

"You're the kind of person who's used to being on the move and is now very secure in being in one place," she said, looking at the clock. "Session over."

"I don't usually dress this well," I said, getting my checkbook out of my bag. "But I'm going to the theater."

"I'm going to the theater, too," she said. Finally! We're on the same wavelength. Get my mother. Quick! It's not too late to have a revelation.

As I walked to her door, we chatted about our favorite plays, about dance, about the opera.

"I hope I helped you," she said, opening her door. I lied and said she had. She probably could see I was lying. Anyone could. "Don't forget to tell your husband to call that guy with the letter D," she said as her door closed.

I walked onto the street into an unexpected rain shower. I ducked into a nearby coffee shop, found a table by the window and ordered a large salad. I pulled out my journal and my pen and proceeded to have lunch with my mother.

The Ghosts of Christmas Past

In a few days, Oliver and I will be going to California to visit his father. I had so hoped this would be the year we'd get to tell him that I'd be giving him a grandchild. I feel embarrassed. His son married a woman that isn't a good breeder.

Before we left on our trip, I called the Office of Reproductive Medicine to find out where we were on the IVF schedule. "Well," the nurse said, "you're not *on* the schedule. And by looking at your last month's FSH level, I'd be the laughing-stock of the hospital if I even called those numbers in!"

I hung up the phone remembering how much I hated her sugary voice from the moment I heard her use the word "scoot" during my first office visit. How could this happen? Last month, when I went for my insemination, they told me I *was* on the list. And now I'm not? Oliver immediately called the doctor's office—first, to let them know how poorly their nurses treat women, and second, to find out what happened. Turns out that one of the doctors—the one that used my name in every sentence—had removed me from the list. I was not a priority case. My FSH was too high.

Whenever I went for my sonograms, I noticed that my name was highlighted in purple on my chart. After the physical exam, I'd pass by the nurses' station and glance at other women's charts. They had yellow lines around their notes. I never had yellow—just purple. I always wondered if the purple lines were a signal to the nurses that meant, "This one's only going through the motions. She's hopeless."

It was enough for me to handle the physical problems. I couldn't handle the business of infertility, too. Oliver called them back again and spoke with the doctor that we liked. He apologized and said he was "unaware of the miscommunication." He agreed to put us back on the list, but informed us that they wouldn't be performing any IVFs until January. And even then, it could be another two to four months before we would be scheduled. There is no way I can count on them again, which is exactly what they counted on. They only wanted candidates who could make their success rates look good.

I tortured myself for not simultaneously signing up with other IVF programs in New York City. I had friends who recommended other programs along the way, but I didn't think it was necessary or even possible to be under the care of two or more programs at the same time. Now that I understand the game, I wish I had hedged my bets.

Oliver has a friend, one of the head doctors at a fertility clinic in California, whom he knew from his years as a medical journalist. We'd been consulting with this doctor by phone, both before and after each of my rounds of stimulation, to let him know how I responded. He told Oliver we were welcome to come to his clinic any time and he would do whatever he could to help us. We quickly made an appointment to see him over the Christmas holidays.

The first Christmas I went with Oliver to visit his father, I thought it would be a nice surprise if we showed up in his dad's driveway with a tree attached to the roof of our rental car. So we went to a tree lot off the Pacific Coast Highway, just a few feet from the beach—already a strange sensation for an Easterner. As the salesman untied several trees for us to inspect, I nodded my head repeatedly as if I understood the difference between a Douglas fir and a Scottish pine. I didn't. I know from latkes and menorahs.

Our next stop was the Trim-A-Tree section in Bullock's department store—a winter wonderland filled with twinkling ornaments, pinecone wreaths, and life-sized ceramic elves.

"Can we get plastic icicles for the tree?" I asked Oliver, filled with the spirit of the season to be jolly.

"I don't like plastic icicles, he said. "I usually stick with metallic globes."

I had been envisioning a tree with more of an assortment. Over the past few years, I'd helped Jeptha and Mary trim *their* trees. In fact, one year, I presented all my non-Jewish friends with ornaments I made out of fancy silk fabric I had left over from my clothing samples. But this was the first tree I'd ever bought.

"Please," I begged, more for the fun of it than caring whether or not we got them. "I *love* icicles."

"We can have icicles on *our* tree," he said.

"We're not having a tree," I said, matter-of-factly. Uh–oh. The frightened look on Oliver's face frightened me. I hadn't said it to be mean. I thought he understood that I was never having a tree. I specifically remembered that, months before, on the coast of Maine, while sitting on lawn chairs sipping beer and eating salsa, Oliver asked me how I felt about dating non-Jewish men. I told him I was planning on having a Jewish home, and as long as the man I dated understood that, there would be no problem.

I was raised in a Conservative Jewish home. My mother kept a kosher kitchen, we observed all holidays, and my brother and I were sent to Hebrew school three times a week well into our teens.

"You can quit if you want to," my mother warned. "But *you* have to tell your grandmother."

My world was Jewish. My street was Jewish, except for the one family who lived at the very end who had eight kids we never knew because they all went to Catholic school. Whenever I dated someone new, my mother would say, "Does this person have a last name?" which was code for, "Is he Jewish?"

Then, in my early twenties, during one of our kitchen conversations, my mother told me she wouldn't be surprised if I married somebody who *wasn't* Jewish. I had no idea what she meant by that. It seems my mother understood a side of me before I did. I needed more than the typical Jewish male could offer.

Once, on a break between my never-ending continuing education classes, I went to visit Jeptha to see if I could live in Colorado. At that time, Jeptha had fallen in love with a man she sat next to on a plane. The two were now living together and she had an empty apartment. In search of my own storybook ending, I went to the snow-peaked mountains of Vail where I finally learned how to ski, hiked up mountains in snowshoes and a backpack, and spent hours reading in the local coffeehouse. After two months, I had a wardrobe of Patagonia sweatshirts, jeans and snow boots purchased at Walmart.

"I can't believe it," I told Jeptha. "I actually don't care what they're wearing in New York.

"I'm not surprised," she said. "You're becoming the real you."

It was in these "road less traveled" places that I fell in love with men who taught me that what you did for a living was less important than how you lived your life. Unfortunately, none of them had ever seen a Jew. One of them, upon seeing my naturally curly hair, asked me if I was one of those "Hebrews." That made me a little nervous. It reminded me that I didn't want to leave my heritage too far behind.

When I returned to New York, I expanded my dating options while becoming a more observant Jew. I took classes in Jewish Law and attended synagogue on all the holidays and most Friday nights. As I became more secure with my Jewish identity, I decided I could date out of my religion because, no matter whom I married, I'd be the keeper of the faith.

Seven months into our relationship, I thought Oliver understood I was never planning to have a tree in any home that we shared. We stood in Bullock's, ornaments in hand, in silence. It was one of those moments that always seem to happen in places like Santa's Workshop or the vegetable aisle in the supermarket. My friend told her mother she was gay next to the K. D. Lang display in a record store.

Oliver bought the box of metallic globes and walked out of the store. The silence continued in the car all the way to lunch. While filling my plate at the salad bar in Carl's Jr., I couldn't contain myself anymore.

"I thought you understood that my being Jewish also meant that I wanted to raise a Jewish family. And Jewish homes don't have trees!" I said, trying to talk and not to cry. "I always thought my kids would go to Hebrew School."

I started thinking about my children growing up without a proper Jewish upbringing, without an understanding of how my parents raised me or who we were as a family. Now I was crying.

People at the register started to stare. Maybe out of concern, or maybe because I was wiping my nose with the same hand that held the spoon everyone used for the low-cal salad dressing. I was also crying because this was the first time Oliver and I were admitting, out loud, that we wanted to marry each other.

"We have time to talk about this," he said, ushering me to a seat. "You act like you've already signed up our children for the Yeshiva."

"Well, maybe this *is* the time to tell you that I like the idea of Hebrew day school and not that after-school agony that I went through."

"Have some fries," Oliver said, which I did, believing I was so upset they couldn't possibly have any caloric value.

When Oliver and I brought the Christmas tree into his father's house, it was late. So, we decided to decorate it after Midnight Mass. I'd always enjoyed participating in rituals other than my own. However, Midnight Mass with the man I might marry was a completely different experience.

I knew Oliver was Catholic. I'd just never considered that, given the proper environment, he would *act* Catholic. He tried to be discreet, but I distinctly saw him accept a wafer and slip it under his tongue. I knew I was being small-minded. After all, he stood beside me on Yom Kippur as I pounded my chest for all the sins I'd committed. Oliver cared enough to learn the prayers he heard on Friday nights. He even sang in Hebrew! This was one night. Yet, in *his* place of worship, I barely opened my mouth but for a few "Amens" that didn't mention anyone's name in particular. I hadn't fully realized that during Midnight Mass, the birth of Jesus Christ would be rejoiced over and over and over again.

My shoulders ached. They felt too heavy for the rest of my body. It must be my Grandmom Ida sitting on them holding a plate of *mandelbrot* while she watched me.

"A *shandeh*! That's what this is," she's saying. "*Feh!*" My Grandpop Abe is here, too, holding whitefish chubs in a brown paper bag like he did every Sunday, looking very disappointed. I remind myself that I am still a nice Jewish girl from Philadelphia. "Sure, a nice Jewish girl," I hear my Grandmom say. "But with a *goyishe* boyfriend!"

Hey! This is no *goy*! This is Oliver. "*Goy*" sounded so much worse than "not Jewish."

The singing got louder and louder. Rounds of hallelujahs filled my head. The priest went up and down the aisles ringing a bell while the praises for Christ got louder. My legs, along with my entire body, started shaking uncontrollably. Was *this* what it felt like when you've accepted Jesus Christ as your savior? I was either having a religious transformation or a nervous breakdown.

Oliver's father was in the row ahead of us. His silver, slicked-back hair reminded me of my Grandpop Harry—same height, same large hands with fingers clutching a prayer book. I remembered standing next to my grandfather in synagogue where he went twice a day. I'd hold his *tallis* bag—the bag that held his fringed prayer shawl—and listen to him recite the *Amidah*. What was I thinking getting serious with someone not Jewish? I was thinking about being with a man whose love of life and sense of family completely filled my empty spaces.

This year, when Oliver and I went to his father's house for Christmas, I came prepared with my own rituals. It was the last few days of Chanukah, so I brought a menorah that was handmade by my father, and also my mother's cookie gun—the kind with metal discs in the shape of trees, snowflakes and stars. While Oliver strung the lights around the tree in the living room, I worked in the kitchen baking Christmas cookies.

"What do you know about making Christmas cookies?" Oliver asked, as I lined them up on the decorative trays that once belonged to his mother.

"Every year my mother and I made cookies for all the kids in her class," I said, remembering our kitchen table covered with trays, sprinkles and dough.

All week, I'd been telling myself that any child we have, however we have that child, would be a part of my family. My grandmother's *kugel*, my mother's cookies—it would all be passed down. But, every morning and every night when I went into the bathroom to wash my face, I stared in the mirror at my cheekbones, the angle of my jaw, my round brown eyes, wondering which parts of me I may never get to see in my child.

"That is such ego!" Oliver said, when I told him I didn't know if I wanted a child if it couldn't be part of me.

"That's why you want to have a child? To reproduce yourself?"

"No, but I want to be related in a literal way. Besides, I did kind of look forward to seeing what a blend of you and me would look like."

"So did I," he said.

The next day, Oliver and I would drive up the coast for an appointment with his friend, the fertility specialist.

Trying

The Season of Hope

When Dr. A. personally drew the blood from my arm, I was amazed. Back in New York, you only saw nurses until the actual consultation. He told me he did this for every one of his patients and I relaxed. Someone was finally on our side.

"So, what do you do Barbara?" he asked, holding my arm, which was going in one direction as my head faced the other. All these months of blood tests and I still couldn't look.

"I'm an artist," I said. "I make performance art videos."

"Oh?" he said, with an emptiness I was used to.

"They're like short films," I said, "only I'm *in* them."

"Uh-huh." Nothing was registering—on his face or from my vein—so I continued.

"I used to be in the garment center," I blurted out, eliminating seven years of my life, a master's degree and a major exhibition, just to give this man something to latch onto for conversation. I *hated* when I did that! After all these years, I still saw myself without a legitimate identity. My behavior made me want to take my crimson test tube, walk out of the office, and come back when I was secure enough to be somebody's mother.

During the consultation, I learned about estradiol. This is a female sex hormone whose number tells the doctors how hard my body is working to keep my FSH down. We had never heard infertility explained this way before. Doctor A. talked to us about the success rates of in vitro fertilization—25% for most women, but lower for me because of my FSH and estradiol levels. He talked about certain couples that choose to try IVF at least once for emotional reasons before moving on. He explained a new, experimental procedure, "cytoplasmic transfer," in which they mix my eggs with another woman's cytoplasm (a material that helps fertilized eggs to implant in the uterus). We would investigate that further when we returned to New York. Finally, he stressed that we might want to start thinking about "options" should my IVF not be successful. This was the day before Christmas and he was going on vacation, so he promised to call us after the New Year to discuss my blood tests.

We drove directly from the doctor's office to a family gathering at the home of Oliver's cousin. We would be meeting her newborn son. Yippee. Thank God she was sympathetic. She was 40, a single mother, and was feeling the pain of having one without the other. She kept reminding us that at least we had each other. *Don't tell me we were turning into one of those couples!* The kind of couple other people admire for being such a great team while the kids of these other people innocently ask, "Why don't Oliver and Barbara have any children?"

"Not now, dear," their mother will say. "I'll tell you when we're in the car."

On the ride back to my father-in-law's home, I was

determined to lose myself in the joys of the holiday season, which begins with the trimming of the tree.

Back East

The phone rang at noon our first day home, but because of jet lag we were just waking up.

"So what's with the baby-making?" asked the voice on the other end. It was one of my friends who knew we had seen another specialist while we were in California. I paused while I tried to remember exactly what Oliver and I had wanted to tell this person about our progress. We tend to tell a different story to each of our friends depending on what they understood about infertility and what we felt comfortable sharing. It's either, "We're still trying, and we feel good about it." Or, for the more knowledgeable, "We're working with a fertility program." For the most infertility-savvy callers, I'd say, "Well, my FSH level is high, but we're hoping to be accepted into one of the IVF programs. In the meantime, we're still inseminating." It's tough. Our friends aren't mere spectators, so vagueness doesn't get too far.

"Do they have you on Clomid?" my friend asked. What about Pergonal? What exactly *is* your FSH?"

"Uh . . . 11.5, but it's not just my FSH that's the problem," I said, pulling myself out from under the covers and propping myself on my elbows. "It's my estradiol."

Oliver was listening and started to wave his index

finger across the front of his neck, signaling me to cut the conversation.

It's hard keeping infertility private when, little by little, my whole world learns that I am trying. My dentist knows because I have to schedule my appointments around my period, in case I need X-rays taken. Now, I just avoid the dentist altogether. My hairdresser knows because, during one visit, he was running late and I had to call my gynecologist from his chair. He also assesses my cappuccino intake. If I accept the frothy beverage, he knows I'm not pregnant or even trying. If I decline, he knows I'm on another cycle. During my last haircut, I had a cappuccino, a diet coke and, by the end of the visit—when he got me talking—a red wine. The woman I go to for facials knows because I innocently told her when Oliver and I first started trying. Now, whether or not fertility is mentioned, my visits have a heaviness of "not yet."

Of course, my brother and his wife know we are trying, but have no idea how difficult trying has become. They just think things are taking longer because of my age. Just before we left on our trip, my sister-in-law innocently asked, "Should we bring up the Prego stroller when we come up to see you for Chanukah?"

"NO," I said. "Do not bring up *anything*. This is going to be a long haul."

The day after New Year's, the doctor from California

phoned with my blood test results. "Happy New Year!" he said. "But when I tell you what I have to tell you, it may not be such a happy new year. Your numbers are too high for me to recommend IVF with our program."

I let Oliver talk to him. I heard what he said. I didn't want to hear the details. Oliver did. Hearing about estradiol levels and success rate percentages helps him emotionally digest the information. Oliver's not a quitter. As soon as he hung up, he began searching the web for a program or a procedure that will help us conceive.

I knew what I had to do. I had to get dressed and go down to Canal Street to see my Chinese herb doctor. A few months before, a professor of mine left a message for me on my answering machine. "Barbara, it's your teacher," she began. "I know you're trying other methods and I don't want to pry, but I just heard about this woman who was told by everyone that she couldn't get pregnant. She went to this man in Chinatown and . . ." I already knew what was coming. "And *after* she had her baby, she got down on her knees and kissed this man's feet!"

I remember the day I heard her message. I'd gone to the Children's Museum to see a Dr. Seuss exhibit with my nephew and niece and had to check my messages to see what dosage of Fertinex I should be administering that evening. As my niece was sitting on Cat in the Hat, I played the message back in my head. I knew exactly whom my teacher was talking about because I'd been to him years before when I was looking to get my energy rebalanced. Despite stories I had heard about his fertility potions, I'd avoided going back because I wanted to be a good girl and obey my doctor by not mixing Western drugs with packets of mysterious Eastern ingredients.

I've had his teas. It's not the kind of tea that fits inside one of those little metal tea balls. I'm talking about dried twigs, berries, seeds, and shreds of what look like the things you pull out of the tread of your boot after a long hike. You brew them for two hours, cool, strain, then refrigerate them and drink three times a day—no sugar. Our house smelled so badly after each brewing that I took to burning toast just to neutralize the kitchen.

As I sat beside my niece on Yertle the Turtle, I wondered why I was bothering with all these injections. All I had to do was go to this herb guy and be saved! Yertle the Turtle. Fertile Myrtle.

"Just call me Fertile Myrtle," my old roommate told me, the last time we spoke. She has two kids and knew we were trying. "Let me know if you need one and I'll pop one out for you," she said. I swear to God, I hate people.

I felt a certain amount of relief deciding to abandon Western medicine and visiting an herbal healer. No appointment needed. I just left my apartment, got on the N train and arrived at the offices of Dr. Fu Zhang. You can't miss his office. There's a huge sign with his name

Trying

painted in large red letters over an arrow the minute you get off the elevator. People are seated in chairs lined up against a wall waiting to see the man behind the white curtain. His desk is only four feet away so you can hear what every one else is telling him. I try not to listen. I focus on what's in front of me—a huge Chinese apothecary with hundreds of drawers that take up an entire wall. In front of the wall is a long counter where another man, the "pharmacist," fills the prescriptions.

This man is a machine. Opening and closing the tiny square drawers—using one hand, sometimes two—he lifts out the prescription: berries, leaves, roots, whatever Dr. Fu Zhang has written down. There are usually about 10 ingredients and he puts them on the table in separate piles. Then he reaches for a stack of paper plates and lines them up in a row. From the separate piles of ingredients, he distributes a handful or so onto each of the plates. Breaking the twigs, ripping the bark, whatever is necessary until all the plates are brimming. Any leftover seeds he gathers up into his hands and throws onto one of the plates. It's not precise, but somehow it's perfect.

Each plate gets poured into its own plastic bag, which he ties into a knot. There will be seven bags in all—enough tea for three weeks. He puts the bags in a larger plastic bag and hands it over to the customer with a nod. Then he moves onto to the next piece of loose-leaf paper with Chinese characters written on it and the performance begins again. Sometimes he takes a break to eat his hot lunch from a thermos. When he eats, he burps loudly.

The doctor came out to get the next person, which would be me.

"Phone number?" he asked. He keeps his patients records in huge loose-leaf books according to phone number.

"I'm already in your book," I tell him, satisfied he'll see I've been here before. Before I became this woman desperate to make a baby.

"What's your problem?" he says.

"I'm trying to get pregnant."

"Ah, O.K." He takes my hand, then gently puts his fingers in a row along my wrist. His eyes are closed. He opens them only to take notes, then closes them again. I like the way his soft fingers feel on my wrist.

"Do you want me to tell you what I know?" I ask. I had no idea how well he understood the English language. It's all done by feel. While he touches my wrist with one hand, the other hand is scribbling rows and rows of Chinese characters, which he tallies at the bottom of each column the way I score a game of scrabble. I attempt to explain my situation. "They tell me my eggs aren't so good."

"You have eggs," he says, ripping off the paper from his pad. "Take now, stop at period."

"You mean I should take the tea *all the time*?" I ask, knowing from my acupuncturist that there are times when you shouldn't take certain herbs. "Even though I might be getting my period in a few days?" I ask, hoping there wasn't a crowd listening in the waiting room.

"Take now, stop at period." he repeats, getting out of his chair and walking me out past the sheeted partition to give the other man the piece of paper with my instructions. There were two people in the waiting area who heard him tell me, "If still not pregnant, come back for more herbs."

I can do this. I will smell up my entire house for months, but I will get pregnant. I kept hearing the voice of the doctor from California. "Happy New Year?!" he joked, as an awkward way of telling me this would be a tough new year for me. I've had worse.

12/31/86

In 1986, I had no date for New Year's Eve. I had a new boyfriend—sort of. But he was away for New Year's—went to Cozumel with his buddies. I didn't care. I could be alone on New Year's Eve. I'd seen the movie "Unmarried Woman" seven times. My desire to move to New York was based on watching Jill Clayburgh and Alan Bates run around Soho.

My neighbor, Alan, had invited me to a party downtown. I told him I would call him if I felt like going out. For now, I was content being with myself for the night. It had been an odd day.

That morning, as I was leaving for work, a policeman greeted me by the elevator on my floor. He asked me which way I was walking when I got out of the elevator. I told him I usually walk up 96th Street to the subway. "Walk up 97th," he said.

Leaving my building, I glanced to the left, saw a sheet covering something large, thought I saw blood, and walked up 97th Street. Later, I found out that a guy on my floor whom I knew from several amiable laundry room encounters had jumped out the window and was lying in front of our building.

When I got to my showroom, the few people that were there were sitting around having coffee. I told them about the man from my building. Then we sat around the showroom taking about how precious life is and naming the people in our lives who were important to us. The names of my parents came easily. A week earlier, while I was on vacation, I'd read a book based on Zen teachings that, as an exercise, told you to make a list of your 10 favorite people. From my hotel room, I called my parents to tell them that they were my top two.

Seven-thirty that night, while sitting in my apartment, the phone rang. It was a friend of mine, Glen. He wasn't a close friend, but someone I knew from the garment center. Glen had recently been in my showroom and known that my parents were going to Puerto Rico on vacation.

"Barb, have you seen the news?" he asked.

Trying

"No."

"I don't want to worry you, but didn't you say your parents were in Puerto Rico?"

"Yes."

"At the Dupont Plaza?"

"Uh-huh."

"Well, I think you should know, the hotel is on fire. They're evacuating."

"Oh my God. Don't even worry about it!" I said, trying to calm him down while I turned on my TV. "My parents were flying out today. Thanks, but I'm totally sure that they left. You must have been *so* scared to call me. Not to worry, though. They're fine!" I told him, as I watched a rescue helicopter helping people evacuate from the burning building.

My Aunt Lee called next.

"Barbie, Sweetie. I'm looking at the television. Didn't your parents say they were staying at that hotel?

"I know all about it, but they're out already," I told her. "Aunt Lee, don't you worry. They had to have left because my father has "airport behavior." He hates to fly, so he always leaves for the airport four to five hours before any given flight—domestic or otherwise. Their flight was late afternoon. They were definitely out."

My father's actions prior to a trip became such a part of our lives. Days before the suitcase came out of the closet, he'd begin removing his socks from the drawer and rolling them up, along with several T-shirts, and placing them in the corner of their bedroom. My mother gave it a name: Airport Behavior.

I fully realized the degree to which this affects him the last time my brother and I drove our parents to the airport.

"Where would you like to go to get a bite to eat with the kids before they drive back?" my mother had asked.

No response.

"Da–ad. Mom asked you where you'd want to eat. Are you hungry?"

No response.

I looked at my mother as her lips mouthed the initials "A. B."

"A. B.?" I whispered.

"Airport behavior," she mouthed, as she pushed me in the direction of the coffee shop.

My Aunt Lee was really my great aunt. My Grandmom Belle's younger sister. Every once in a while, she'd call me to see how my life in New York was working out. She loved telling me about the days she worked for Mr. Hearst as a secretary for one of his magazines. If my aunt heard I was dating someone, she'd call me up to say, "Should I buy my shoes yet?" which was her way of asking if there would be a wedding in the near future. Of all my grandmother's sisters, Lee and my mother always felt a special connection. Maybe she felt something—had a premonition. I didn't.

Trying

Two a.m. The phone woke me up. It was Joan, the daughter of the couple with whom my parents were vacationing—our back-to-back neighbors, Bernie and Anita.

"Barb, my father just called," she said. I was already feeling relieved. "My mother and your parents were in the casino when a bomb went off. I think you'd better come home to Philadelphia. I just spoke to your brother. We're all flying to Puerto Rico tomorrow night."

"I'm staying *here*," I said. "My mother would totally call me here."

Early the next morning, my brother called me. "Get on the train, now," he said nervously.

"O.K. I'll come," I told him. I decided to go, not because I thought they were dead, but because it would be nice to be with my brother when our parents called us.

"Barbie, I am so–o–o sorry," my mother would say. "What a tremendous misunderstanding. You must have been just sick about it."

I packed some T-shirts, jeans, a bathing suit, a black dress and—for some strange reason—photos of my parents for identification purposes. I was on an adrenaline rush. It felt like I was watching somebody else's made-for-TV movie. It was almost fascinating.

I walked into Penn Station, glanced at the *New York Post* headline that read BOMB IN PUERTO RICO, 96, DEAD, and got on the train. Ever since my father's surgeries, I was used to getting on a train when I didn't know what I'd face on the other end. I'd put on my Walkman, stare out the window and, just like when I was younger, watch the train tracks merge into one another. This time, when I got to my brother's apartment, my Uncle Norman—my father's brother—was sitting on the couch with his head in his hands. I sat on the floor and looked into the part of his face I could see behind his fingers.

"You're going go have to go down there," he said.

"What?"

"You and David are going to have to go down to Puerto Rico and look for your parents."

"What do you mean *look*?" I said. "What am I, Colombo?" I pictured myself searching through the rubble, tripping over fire hoses, lifting up furniture, looking for my parents.

My brother's phone kept ringing. There were friends who gave us numbers of people they knew in Puerto Rico who might help us. An old boyfriend of mine. Even my old boss from Philadelphia who had just seen the evening news.

"Please tell me there are two Barbie Nuddles," he said.

"There aren't."

I realized the numbers flashing on the television with Emergency Phone numbers and the Red Cross Office were for us. We were flying out within an hour.

Six of us went to the airport. My brother David, my cousin Morton, myself, and Bernie and Anita's two daughters, Joan and Amy. I could barely see out the window of the car because of all the snow.

On the plane, I started eating as soon as the stewardess came by with our snacks. "They're fine, Joan. I know it!" I insisted, waving my cheese sandwich in the air. "Really." After all, I would know. I was into metaphysics. I even slept with crystals. If anyone would know if our parents were dead, I would. I bit into the thick layers of American cheese on white bread. I figured if Morton saw me eating, he'd think I was O.K. That I wasn't worried.

Staring into the blank sky, I decided that if something worse had happened—if my parents were horrifically burned or something—I'd rather they be dead. And if one was dead, I wanted them both to be gone. I didn't think I could handle only one surviving.

We arrived at night, it was hot, and everything felt more confusing in the dark. We took a taxi to an apartment owned by friends of Bernie and Anita. Bernie was standing in the driveway the moment our car pulled in. I watched Joan and Amy hug their father when we got out. Once inside, he introduced us to Michael and Mary Casello, the people who opened up their home to us.

"Your parents are lovely, lovely people," Mary said, pressing my face into her cheek. She left the room crying. Bernie sat down and immediately started telling us about the week he'd spent with my parents.

"We had a wonderful vacation," he said. "If we could

just get my wife to stop all that damn shopping." And then, turning to my brother and me, "And your mother to stop talking. 'Take a breath, Roz!' That's all I said the whole week, Barbie, I swear. That woman doesn't come up for air." He made a point of telling us that, for their next trip, they were planning to take a cruise.

I started wondering why Bernie was taking the time to tell us all of this? Weren't we wasting time? We should be calling people. He should be filling us in on all the facts of the accident. It was three o'clock in the morning. I was exhausted from the long day, but we listened for another hour until Bernie finally began to speak about the incident. All four of them had been in the casino using up their chips before riding to the airport. Their bags were packed and sitting in the lobby. Bernie left to use the men's room. There was an explosion. He ran back towards the doors of the casino and they had already been locked shut. We learned later that the explosion had been the result of a fire set by disgruntled hotel employees who wanted to terrorize Puerto Rico's tourist trade.

"It doesn't look good," Bernie said. "I spent the morning at the Red Cross station and the afternoon calling all the local hospitals. We can do more tomorrow." He never came out and said the words. No one did—for days. Joan and Amy sensed that their mother was dead. My brother believed the worst had happened, too. I didn't.

At night, I shared the bed with Joan and Amy. My

Trying

brother slept on the floor to my left. I couldn't cry. No one else was crying. If I cried, I'd break the silence. I stared up at the ceiling instead.

"Mom," I said silently. "Can you hear me? Tell me where you are and we'll find you." I waited. Then I asked, "Mom, are you dead?" I held my breath and listened with my heart. I felt only one word—"Yes."

The next morning, I woke up in this strange bed in Puerto Rico. I was the last to be dressed. I stared at my duffel bag and seriously wondered, "What do you wear to search for your dead parents?" I decided I'd pretend to be Angie Dickinson from *Police Woman* for the entire day. I watched this show when I was a teenager. I hadn't thought of it since. Every week, Angie fought crime in tight jeans and little white sneakers. She had a little bit more of a bust than me but, nevertheless, I was Angie and she was me.

We were instructed to call Centro Medico, the largest local hospital, because they had the best burn unit. I dialed the number, was put on hold for five minutes, then someone else put me on hold for five more. When a nurse finally came on the line, she asked me which part of the hotel my parents were in. I told her "the casino," and she kept me on hold even longer. It was six days before I learned that no one in the casino had survived.

The waiting is what makes you crazy. Back then, Amy and I kept each other company for hours by exploring the contents of each other's pocketbooks while we sat at the Red Cross station. A few afternoons, they sent us away by 3 o'clock. "No more news until the next day." Another *day*? At night, we would go out to dinner and share stories—lots of stories—about our parents' lives. It kept them alive a little longer.

Why can't I remember those anxious days in Puerto Rico as I'm kept on hold waiting for my latest FSH results? When Little Miss "I'd-Be-the-Laughing-Stock-of-the-Hospital" makes me feel like shit for having too high of an FSH level. I was actually afraid of talking to this nurse. Whenever she picked up my call, I'd ask her to immediately connect me to the doctor.

"He may be a while," she'd say, putting me on hold.

"Fine, I'll wait." I'd say. You have no idea how I can wait.

While my brother and I were in Puerto Rico, we had to fill out physical identification forms. "Mommy, 5'7", 140 pounds," I began. "And she has a beauty mark over her left pelvic bone."

"How do *you* know?" my brother asked.

"She's my mother," I said. I'd seen that mark for years whenever I talked to her while she stood naked, still wet from the shower, as she searched her dresser drawer for a pair of stockings without a run in them. I also noticed her beauty mark every time I accompanied her into Gimbel's dressing room, helping her try on, as she called them, "outfits." My mother's beauty mark was on that bulge, the round and puffy part below the waistband of her stockings. The bulge wasn't her fault, she would say. "It's just what happens to you after you have a baby." These days, I wonder if I'll be lucky enough to have that same bulge.

Seven days after my parents died, while flying home from Puerto Rico with their bodies stowed below, a flight attendant came by with lunch. Suddenly, the plane jerked sideways and my tray, along with all its contents, spilled onto my lap. Lesson number one after a tragedy: just because something horrific happens to you doesn't mean nothing *else* bad will happen to you.

Bagels and Blood Tests

Oliver and I aren't giving up hope. There are other programs in New York and New Jersey, and another program in Virginia that we'd heard about from friends of friends (none of our closest friends had experienced this level of infertility).

Last Sunday morning, we went to register with one of the top IVF centers on our list. Each program usually likes to do its own blood work so it meant I had to endure another round of tests. I particularly hated it when day three of my cycle fell on a Sunday. The fertility clinic is packed with couples reading the Sunday *Times* and drinking Starbucks coffee. I'm surprised they don't hand out lox and bagels. When they finally call my name, I'm led to a room where there's a line-up of women sitting with their arms stretched out.

My arm has been jabbed dozens of times since last summer, when it all started. And I understand that finding a usable vein is difficult. My veins are thin and the one on my right arm "rolls." I've even learned to tell them to use a thin needle, to make their job easier. I'm usually very patient. However, this morning, the nurse taking blood from me is on a search and destroy mission in my arm. Normally, I never look at my arm once the needle is in. But this nurse kept fishing under my skin, pushing deeper and deeper and getting nowhere.

"Stop!" I finally said. "Take it out of my arm NOW!"

"I'll get another nurse," she said.

Another nurse came over and extracted blood without any problem. "Is she new?" I whispered, referring to nurse number one.

"Yes, but she's done this many times."

"Yeah, well . . ." I didn't want to say anything more. I wasn't even in their program, yet. But I couldn't help rolling my eyes.

As I waited for my paperwork to come back, I looked around to see how the other women were doing. One was seated near me ready to leave but waiting for information none of the nurses had time to give her. That was partly my fault. She was still waiting because her nurse stopped to help me.

Trying

"I'm so nervous," she said.

"Tell me about it," I said. "I'm very sorry you're still waiting because of me."

"It's O.K.," she said. I got up to leave and, as I passed her, she looked at me knowingly and said, "It's all worth it." She had an accent. Later, when I thought about it, I wasn't sure if she had said, "It's all work," or "It's all worth it." I told Oliver what happened.

"Why would she say it's all *work*?" he asked.

"Because it is."

Finally, I was feeling much better. I slept well. Oliver and I had a great date. We went to a David Mamet play, then out to dinner afterwards at our favorite French bistro. Oliver and I shared a bottle of wine as we talked about the play. It was one o'clock in the morning when we finally left the restaurant, came home, and made love—not a baby. Nice.

Not for long.

There's a child's toy that involves using a hammer to bang a wooden block into a hole of the same size and shape. I feel like the piece of wood that gets banged repeatedly into the wrong hole. When the nurse from our latest IVF center called today with my results, she simply said, "You're abnormal."

"What does that mean?" I asked.

"You're results are out of our ballpark."

I pictured my FSH printed on the side of a baseball

flying over the fence at Yankee Stadium. What is wrong with nurses? I could not believe this kind of language was coming from someone with ovaries. She read me the number. I was stunned. It was nearly twice as high as any previous test. I told her that number seemed unusually high.

"Are you on withdrawal from any drugs?" she asked.

"No," I said. "Not since November." I didn't mention the wood pulp beverage prescribed by my acupuncturist because it had been over a month since I last drank it, and I hadn't even started my next round of Chinese teas. But I knew one thing: I'd be turning my kitchen into an herbal brewery that evening.

Then the nurse explained that their lab uses a reference range different from some other labs, meaning their "20" could be someone else's "12." But, either way, it was still too high for them.

It's times like this when I'm sorry I left my job in the garment center. You hang up clothes, you speak with limitless enthusiasm about the virtues of pink or teal, and you make lots of money. I was good at that. Right now, I'd like to feel good at something.

Next, Oliver and I decided to call the program in New Jersey that Doctor A. in California had told us about—the one doing cytoplasm transfers. The problem with my eggs, according to him, is that they may be too weak—unable to implant and grow on their own. In a cytoplasm transfer, a portion of the cytoplasm—the fluid surrounding the nucleus from a healthy (i.e. donor) egg—is collected and used to replace the substances in the less healthy egg (i.e. mine). Translation: I'd get to keep my gene pool! I can live with that.

Oliver spoke to the head nurse and we have an appointment for a consultation the second week in March. That's over a month away, but this could be what saves me. It's a progressive, complicated, experimental procedure, but well within my capacity to endure if, in the end, it gets me what I want. I prayed we'd have the chance to try. I counted the days to our appointment.

Another Chapter

How Would You Like Your Eggs?

The other day, I was in the bathroom at the New York City Ballet. As I waited for a free stall, I watched a young girl of six or seven, in a black velvet dress and tights, standing in front of the mirror admiring her hair. She wore it pulled back in a bun like a ballerina. The girl seemed tall for her age, as I had been. I wondered what her mother looked like. And then I had this thought. How would I feel if someone came into this bathroom right now and said to me, "The mother of this little girl is terminally ill. She can no longer care for her and wants to know if you would like to take her daughter home with you?"

Could I love her as my own? Could I do that?

If Oliver and I choose to adopt, I could have the daughter I've always wanted. But she'd have nothing of me in her—at least nothing physical. I know it's unrealistic to think I could select which features I would pass on. I know there are no guarantees with a natural child. But I keep wishing to give someone my long legs, which is ironic because, for the majority of my adolescence, I despised them.

When I was a teenager, I hated my height. Every night, I'd go to bed and pray to God to make me shorter. "And God," I'd pray. "If you were wondering how you could do this, I think that removing some bone in the space between my ankle and my calf would be O.K."

The summer I turned 16, I went to Israel as part of my Jewish education. Visiting the Western Wall was one of the most anticipated excursions of our trip. At the sacred remains of this first Jewish Temple, people come to pray, to wish, to mourn. While everyone in my group stood at the Western Wall writing notes to their dead grandmothers and slipping them in the spaces between the bricks, I wrote a note to God asking him to make me shorter. I wanted to date Saul Levitt, a guy on my trip who was a head shorter than I was.

It was during my painful teenage years that I decided I should try and marry someone short—but not too short.

Trying

My height. Nothing taller. That way, when we had children, I would reduce the chances of having an extremely tall girl. I didn't want her to suffer the way I did, by being taller than every boy. Especially every Jewish boy I knew.

"You're not a little girl," my mother warned me as I stood, slump-shouldered, in the dressing room of Lord and Taylor's. "But that doesn't mean you're not pretty."

I was thin, able to slip my already 5-foot, 8-inches into every designer jean, maxi coat or mini skirt. But I'd have traded it all for a few less inches. It wasn't until college that I started to feel more comfortable with my height, and by the time I moved to New York, everyone on the streets of Manhattan seemed tall. But by then, I didn't care.

When doctors tell me I might need to find someone else's eggs, I say, no! Not possible. I keep thinking about when I was younger, lying in my parent's bed with them and watching TV. I'd put my feet right up against my father's so we could show my mother how our big toes were exactly the same. I want that. I want *something*.

While waiting to find out if cytoplasm transfer would be our salvation, I went to see my gynecologist for a regular checkup. I hadn't been there since he referred me to a fertility specialist almost a year ago. I'd forgotten that in the midst of infertility there is still the matter of a regular PAP smear. The thought of pulling my pants down one more time exhausted me. And I dreaded sitting in the waiting room on Fifth Avenue filled with happy pregnant women and advertisements for *Parent* magazine and diaper services. At the end of my exam, I sat in my doctor's office and filled him in on my fertility treatments.

"It seems I went from 'trying' to 'your eggs may not be good enough' in two seconds," I said, trying to be funny, but desperate for him to show me a way out of all this.

He rolled his chair away from his desk, took a deep breath, and looked at me. "I want to tell you something," he said, with the soft voice of a man used to delivering babies. "At two in the morning, when the baby is resting on your shoulder after a feeding or you need to quiet him from crying, it's *your* baby. Where it came from doesn't matter."

I stared at this man in a white coat, who, as he spoke, pretended to nuzzle a baby on his shoulder. Something happened. I saw the baby! I could *feel* the baby, *my* baby, in a way that had nothing to do with eggs, or sperm, or FSH.

"The sooner you get a family, however you choose to do it," he said, "you'll feel better."

He talked to me about adoption. He explained that if I was concerned that it should be an Eastern European (my ancestry) baby, he could help me with that. He also gave me the name of an IVF program that specializes in egg donation.

"There is a long wait list for both," he warned. "It

could be up to a year. So, even as you're trying and waiting to see about these other IVF programs, it wouldn't hurt to get your name onto these lists."

The day before Valentine's Day, Oliver and I went to meet the doctor who was recommended by my gynecologist. Another introduction. Another push forward. Another office with a sprawling view of Central Park. Upon scanning the waiting room, I noticed a coffee station that I figured was for the nurses. But when the receptionist handed me the patient information form to fill out, she said, "Help yourself to something warm to drink."

"Thank you," I said. I think I will. Let's just drop the pretense that caffeine is keeping me from getting pregnant. In fact, I'm here to learn about using someone else's eggs. I think I'll have myself a big ol' cup of coffee!

I stared at two freshly brewed pots—decaffeinated and regular. I chose decaf. Just in case.

The doctor was young. You know how people say you can tell you're getting old when your doctor seems too young to be practicing? This guy was close. I noticed a photograph of his wife and kids behind his desk. They must have started early. You see, even as Mr. Too-Young-To-Be-a-Doctor was immersed in medical school, he knew enough to start a family. And now he was making a fortune helping women like me.

Oliver and I sat in his office and chatted with the doctor about the art deco poster behind his desk, his newly expanded facilities, and about the doctor that referred us to him. I filled him in on my fertility history. Then, looking up from his notepad, he said, "And why are you, uh . . . what are you hoping to, uh . . . what can I tell you about us?" I think he was afraid to end his question because he knew my response might bring on tears.

"I'm here because I need to investigate egg donation," I said. Some tears. I took a tissue and a piece of hard candy from the jar on his desk.

Oliver jumped in to tell the doctor we were also investigating other IVF programs and insemination treatments. I didn't really want to mention any other programs because consultations feel like interviews. I don't want them to know I'm courting other possibilities. I want them to think they are my only hope so they will try, as hard as they can, to help me.

The doctor began describing his IVF program as well as the donor selection process. Oliver and I would be able to request skin color, hair color, height, weight, and even interests. As he spoke, I'm calm. I'm beyond calm. My head isn't anywhere near my heart. It's in a Honda dealership choosing interior seat colors and other available options. In six months to a year, we'd drive away with a new model. That's how long the wait-list is for donor eggs—*once you register*. This was only the consultation.

I was in such shock that I started to imagine how nice it might be to pick a beautiful Czechoslovakian girl with dark eyes and even longer legs than mine. This was better than using my genes! I'll pick a real beauty. Yeah, I'll pick some gorgeous woman to make a child with my husband.

This sucks. No matter what my gynecologist said about ". . . at two in the morning it will be my baby," I'm getting cheated. At that moment, the thought of using a donor felt like choosing a woman with whom my husband would have an affair.

I wondered how Oliver felt about sharing a child with a woman he never met. What if Oliver got curious about where this woman lived? His whole life, he'd wonder if he'd seen her at the movies, or in our local diner, or seated next to him on the subway. Finally, the mystery would overwhelm him and he would find her address. They'd meet over coffee to discuss the baby. They'd share photos, childhood stories. They'd have another cappuccino—a double, and the next thing you know, I'm packing my bags so they can move in together and raise *their* child.

What would an egg donor do to our marriage? Would I be jealous of the genetic connection my husband had with our child? One day, as they laughed uncontrollably at a television show whose humor escaped me, would I get up and leave the room, yelling, "She's not mine anyway!"

The doctor needed to record my family history. This is the portion of every new medical consultation that, no matter how casual I try to sound, brings the conversation to a more intimate level than I would like.

"Family illnesses." he began. "Mother's side?"

"High blood pressure," I said. "But nothing big."

"Father's?"

"He had several benign brain tumors removed, but he was fine."

"Are they living or deceased?"

"Deceased," I said. He looked confused.

"In an accident," I said, wanting to keep it brief. Oliver watched my face as I went through the fact-finding ritual with yet another doctor.

"That's horrible."

"Yes, it is," I said, not wanting to visit just how horrible. "So you see," I said, taking a deep breath. "It's very important that, if I *were* to use a donor, I need to find someone who is *exactly* like me so that I can carry on my Jewish genes as well as my physical characteristics." Now I'm crying.

He explained that Jewish donors are extremely hard to come by. "High demand and, truthfully," he confessed, "not that many Jewish women are willing to donate their eggs to make money. The wait could be up to a year."

Fine. I'll wait. By then, I'll have gotten pregnant on my own or killed myself.

I explained to him that being an interfaith couple made finding a Jewish donor very important to me. I was sure this nice, young, Jewish doctor was thinking I should have thought of that when I got married. By now, my grandmother was perched on the art deco poster with her head in her hands. *I just want you to have whatever it is that you want.*

"Take another tissue," the doctor said, passing me the box. "We buy these at the Price Club."

"I've already cried my way up Fifth Avenue," I said, wiping my tears.

"Hopefully, this will be your last stop," he says, sympathetically.

It better not be.

"Don't you wish you married someone with better eggs?" I asked Oliver when we got home. As if I was rating myself at the 4-H agricultural fair. "How would you feel about mixing your sperm with someone else's eggs?"

"Look, of course, I'd be disappointed," he said. "I want to be able to see someone with your eyes, your legs, your smile. But those are not the things I married you for. It's your personality, your sense of humor. Our child's view of the world."

I tried to let his words sink in. They were good. All good, which is how Oliver is about all of this. That's Oliver. Mr. Good Guy. Well, if I did use a donor, at least Oliver would see a part of himself in his—I mean *our* child. Oliver would never want me to do it for that reason. But for me, that would be the reason.

"It means much more to me if our kid is going to

laugh like you," Oliver said, "than if you have the same hair color. Besides, how many kids do we know that look like their parents?"

His words brought temporary relief. Until I walked down the street and saw the hundreds of children that do.

Calgon, Take Me Away

I need air. I opened all the windows in our apartment and suddenly flashed on the nights in my old apartment—the one I had when I was single. I'd wake up short of breath, panicked, afraid to close my eyes and return to sleep. If I closed my eyes, I thought I would forget to breathe. Other times, I'd wake up and find my T-shirt soaked with sweat. I'd always thought it was due to nerves, post-traumatic stress, or eating that green apple before bedtime. Maybe they were anxiety attacks. Maybe they were hot flashes. Perhaps I was experiencing perimenopause—a condition one of my doctors had mentioned was possible. Had I been ignoring the signs?

It was 30 degrees outside. Usually, I find any temperature below 50 *freezing*. But today, I took a walk from 101st Street to a store on 77th to exchange a shower curtain. They had given me a frosted one, when I'd specifically asked for clear. I walked fast. That way, the wind would smack my face and numb my ears and head. Ah, numb. I've been here before. Welcome.

Trying

* * *

For Valentine's Day, Oliver and I had a beautiful dinner at home. I found a recipe for a romantic dinner for two in a food magazine I read in my chiropractor's office. I spent the whole day shopping for and preparing veal chateaubriand to be served alongside a frisée salad with warmed bacon dressing. As the strips of meat began sizzling in the pan, I realized this was the first time in my life that I'd ever cooked bacon. I consider myself relatively kosher based on my upbringing, but I guess I was looking for a thrill.

The food portion of the evening was exciting. However, my sex drive was becoming as weak as my eggs. I don't feel in love. I feel like a broken body. A fraud—fertile on the outside, barren on the inside.

I wake up consumed with emptiness. I've reached the point I've heard other infertile women talk about reaching. I don't want to go out of my apartment at three o'clock because my street is jammed with mothers picking their kids up from school. If I see an older mother with a baby, especially if she has twins (a clue that fertility drugs were used), I can't help wonder how old she is. Is she going to run after her child if he reaches the busy intersection before she does? Can she still run?

I'm bored. I am grossly aware of the passage of time. It goes very slowly when you're in between fertility treatments, waiting day-by-day for a new cycle to begin. I need the months to fly by until all this is over and I can get in line for the swing, just like the other mothers at the playground.

One weekday, I decided to face my fears and went to the playground to meet my friend and her daughter. She was late. As I walked around the jungle gym on my own, I saw someone I knew.

"What are *you* doing here?" she said, holding her child's hand as he went down the slide.

"I'm waiting for a friend," I said. Suddenly, I felt like someone had set up a velvet rope outside Hippo Park and I wasn't allowed in without a kid. Of course, the woman didn't mean anything by it. But lately, I've been overreacting to things people say, and that vulnerability is making me nuts.

Weekends don't provide the relief they used to, either. Oliver and I have done it all before. Saturday morning breakfasts at Metro Diner. Movies followed by a late night dinner at Café Luxembourg. Sundays in Riverside Park leisurely reading the *New York Times*. Done. Done. Done. We're supposed to be exhausted and complaining about 3 a.m. feedings by now.

I want to be my old self—my single self. I want my wild curly hair and my motorcycle boots. I want to smoke. I desperately want thoughts of something exciting to take over my mind—a play, a foreign movie, perhaps a kiss from someone new.

The past few days, I've been fantasizing about making

love with a painter I met at an exhibition. He lives in my neighborhood. He's divorced and has an adorable son who looks just like him. It hurts me to see the face of this man reflected in his son. I'm not sure I'll ever get that. It makes me crazy. Look at him. Look at his son. They are so great together. He's such a great artist. He's asked me to photograph some of his work. He totally likes me. Wow. If I left my marriage and married him, we could be a family already!

When I was single, I never wanted to go out with anyone who was divorced, let alone someone with a kid. No matter how old I was getting, when it came to being a parent, I wanted it to be the first time for the both of us. But if I knew I'd have this much trouble conceiving, I wouldn't have limited the playing field. I'd have let myself fall in love with some cute, newly divorced father and, together, we would have made a child of our own by now. I have made all the wrong choices. Damn. I usually wait until nighttime to let my mind go *this* far.

Enough! I promised her that I'd call if I ever needed help again, and I do.

I hadn't been to my therapist in over a year, but I knew it was time. It was beyond time. I had tried to call her a few months earlier but her answering service picked up and said that she had taken a "leave of absence." Her service gave me a number in case of emergency. The number gave a Westchester area code. I thought it must be her home number. I decided she'd taken a leave of absence because she became a mother. I didn't know if she'd become a mother. I never called. I just imagined her sitting in her kitchen next to the food processor, feeding her baby homemade jars of peas and carrots. She'd be so filled with the glow of motherhood that I couldn't bear telling her that I was afraid I didn't love Oliver enough, and that I wondered if I should leave him before we have any kids. Oh, and by the way, I'm infertile.

This time when I called, she was back in her office. I didn't want her to think I was calling to rehash my issues of mother loss. I told myself that, deep in my heart, there was no one besides Oliver who I'd rather go through any of this with. So I got right to the fertility part.

"This is *me*," I kept saying. "How sick is it that, after all I've been through, I might not be able to have a kid? How can this be happening to me? Can you believe that the girl who lost her mother now can't become one? What am I supposed to learn from this?"

"Stop thinking that you have lessons to learn and that's why you need to struggle," she told me. "The struggle sucks and if you *had* gotten pregnant, you'd be enjoying your life and you wouldn't be thinking about lessons. Allow yourself to feel miserable. It *is* miserable."

"No," I said. "I can't. I won't. I was depressed for too long."

"Unlike what you went through in the past, though,

this will have an end," she assured me. "You *will* get a baby. *However* it is you get a baby."

But I wanted to *have* a baby, not get one.

"There's something else," I said, realizing we had a little time left until next week's session. And there would definitely be a next week. "I'm having the wildest sex dreams of my life. And none of them involve Oliver. I think it's a sign. Have you ever heard me talk about sexual fantasies before? Me?"

"No. Not very often," she said. I think I saw her laughing.

"Well, there's this painter that I know and I can't stop thinking about him. I mean, I want to sleep with the guy. I mean it. I can really see myself doing it."

"Barb, many women fantasize about having an affair when they're having difficulty conceiving. They feel as if they deserve to live out a fantasy as a trade-off for what they are going through."

"So, I'm having a normal reaction?" I laughed, happy to be normal in some area of my life.

"Very," she added.

"Are you attracted to him?"

"Well, in some ways, I feel this strong connection. But I don't know. He's not exactly my type."

"Good!" she said, seizing my last words. "You need to keep telling yourself that. Don't do it. Do not do anything," she repeated. "I'll see you next week."

As I got up to leave, she stood up with me. "Barb. This is not like the other losses. You will get a baby."

First Love (a baby one)

I experienced my first pangs of wanting to have a baby when I was 31. I'd gone to Colorado to visit Jeptha and her 3-month-old daughter, Calloway, for Christmas. My first day or two, all I could do was watch Jeptha watch over Callie as she nursed her, changed her, or as she just lay on the sofa between us as we talked. I couldn't believe that she had done it. Amazing. My best friend had a child—a daughter, just like she'd always wanted. One night, Jeptha was busy making dinner and Callie needed to be changed. I, never one to volunteer to water other people's plants, found myself saying, "I'll do it."

Calloway smiled and waited patiently as I figured out which direction the diaper and the adhesive tapes were supposed to face. I loved holding her soft tiny legs as I lifted her up and settled her back inside a fresh diaper. She trusted me. I was falling in love. WAIT! These feelings of baby bliss are SO not me. I was never the type of woman to run over to other people's babies and make ridiculous cooing noises, or ask to hold any newborn that was in the arms of someone I knew. But Calloway got to me, especially as I watched her shut her eyes and fall into a happy sleep.

That night, I awoke restless from my own growing

pains. I loved being a part of Jeptha's new life, but what was I doing with mine? We had both quit our jobs in the garment center to find happiness. She found hers. I was still floundering on the road less traveled. At the time, I was taking some classes and I think I was dating someone who was, as my mother used to say, "remarkably nondescript." I lay in bed feeling alone and sad. I kept telling myself to think about Callie. This baby only sees the peace in the world. She feels the love of everyone around her and she slumbers to it. I realized how incredibly happy she made me feel. She was my new symbol for what feeling something for someone could be like. Then I fell asleep.

The summer after Calloway was born, Jeptha had bought a guest ranch with her husband. New baby. New business. New husband. Jeptha called to say she needed my help. "Besides," she insisted, "life on a ranch is an experience you shouldn't miss." I'd be starting graduate school in the fall and decided that photographing cowboys would be good for my portfolio. I learned later that cowboys work with cows and *wranglers* work with horses. That was the first of many lessons I was about to learn.

I loved pushing Calloway in her stroller around acres of land covered with sage bushes. I felt humbled by the hugeness of the mountains and found tremendous peace walking beneath them. It was hard for me to be neurotic when there was so much nature for my mind to absorb. As Calloway and I made our way along dirt roads, occasionally greeted by a roaming longhorn (not exactly the traffic I was used to), I sang her all my old camp songs. After I performed the final stanza to "Sippin' Cider Through a Straw," I moved on to Jethro Tull's "War Child," Van Morrison's "Moondance," and the Beatles' *White Album*. It was on those dusty roads that I realized that I could be myself *and* be a mother. With Calloway perched on my hip, I'd make up the cabin beds, answer phones, or greet incoming guests.

By now, Calloway was nine months old and hadn't yet learned to crawl. I worried that she wasn't crawling because there were no other babies around for her to watch. So, every day, I went around Jeptha's living room on all fours to show her how. I imagined what it might be like with a daughter of my own.

Cowboys Are My Weakness

That summer was filled with a lot of firsts. I never thought I'd own a real cowboy hat. I never thought I'd drive cattle. I never thought I'd sleep with a cowboy—I mean a wrangler.

My first week at the ranch, Rick and Everett—two of the wranglers in charge of trail rides—drove me to a Walmart (a 50-minute trip) to buy a white straw cowboy hat. That's what real wranglers wore in the summer. Using spit and the heat of his hand, Everett shaped the sides of my new hat. Then he put it on my head and flicked the front rim with his fingers to see if it was snug. I would have laughed out loud if they weren't so serious about the whole ritual.

As for riding horses—they scared me. Other than a pony ride at Adventureland Day Camp when I was eight, I'd never even been on a horse. They were big, and I didn't have a clue how to make them go. I also feared that they'd break for the border the second I was in the saddle. I tried to view my summer at the ranch as part of a phobia-reduction program. In the morning, I'd force myself to go down to the stables and help feed them. Eventually, I tagged along on trail rides, where all you had to do was sit on the horse and chat it up with the guests. I tried to look casual. I don't know if I succeeded. By the time I went on my first cattle drive, which is a much faster ride that requires following horses that are following cattle, I wanted to get some feedback on my riding.

"Did ya fall off?" the head wrangler asked.

"No."

"Then you're fine."

Breakfast was at 7:30, after the wranglers tacked down the horses. Annie, the cook, made great omelets (when she was in a good mood—I mean, sober). I liked Annie. We bonded one night when she told me about the time her father lay dying in an intensive care unit and she sang him the song *Danke Schön* using a coat hanger as a microphone.

One morning, at the end of our long dining table, I noticed a wrangler who winced with every bite he took.

"That's Chris," Everett said. "He rolled his truck last night."

Chris was 17. And 17 years—to anyone who's grown up in McCoy, Colorado—is a lifetime. He had a rough family situation and was considered by the state to be an emancipated minor by the time he was 12. One night, Annie and Everett invited me out to the local bar. Chris was coming, too, even though he was too young to drink. But he could shoot pool.

"I won me my truck with this," he said, tucking a small case inside his jacket as we walked through the door. "Never let them see you have your own stick," he warned. "You pull it out when you have to."

When you asked Chris how tall he was, he'd answer cowboy-style, "Six-two with my boots on."

"*I'd* sleep with him, but I'm married," Jeptha told me on one of our hour-long rides to the nearest market to stock up on baby food for Callie or hoof cream for the horses.

I don't know if I slept with Chris because I really wanted to, or because I was making up for all the times in my life when I said no when I really meant yes. But, once in your life, every woman should be with a man who says, before he gets into bed, "Just a second, honey. I need to take my spurs off."

One time, Chris drove us out to an abandoned

copper mine to see the blue-green rock formations on the walls. We pulled up to a heavy wire fence that was meant to block trespassers, but there was a small hole cut into it just big enough to slide through.

Chris reached under the seat cushion of his truck and grabbed a flashlight and a shotgun, which was as long as one of his legs. "Just in case there's somethin' in there meaner than I am," he said, loading one bullet and shoving four more into his pocket.

"Oh, sure," I said. Like I'd ever seen a loaded shotgun, let alone needed to use one. I got out of the truck and, with my hat in my hand, followed Chris and crawled through the hole. Only he kept his hat on. He never took his hat off, except when he slept or if the wind took it while he was roping cattle. I stayed right behind him because it was so dark in the cave, you could only see where he pointed his flashlight. One time, he took a quick turn and I was left in what felt like the darkness of eternity, wondering how far I could walk into the blackness before I'd have to call his name.

Then I heard him. "Lookie! Lookie! Lookie!" he yelled. "Over here! There's an *itty-bitty* stream that goes right along this track." If Chris knew how cute he sounded using that phrase, he'd stop using it.

I knew I might regret my behavior. But on the other hand, this was an adventure. And as I tried to piece my life back together, adventures were all I was after. One evening, as we sat by a fire made with branches of cherry wood from a neighboring orchard, Chris asked me, "How much is your rent?"

"Why?" I said, not wanting to tell him about the overpriced rents in New York City.

"Move here," Chris said, staring into the flames. "I'll take care of you. And next summer you can ride Fancy. And if she's not big enough, I'll let you have Bayhorse."

I'd been on Bayhorse the day Chris took Jeptha and me on what we still refer to as "the ride of our lives." Chris was fearless, and when I was with him, I rode that way, too. For the moment, staying in Colorado sounded like a good idea.

One morning at the ranch, as Chris and I got out of bed, I heard the song "Stairway to Heaven" playing on the radio—a song I remembered listening to when I was Chris's age. It suddenly became clear that this was *his* adolescence, not mine.

In The City of Brother Love

That same summer, another baby entered my life—my nephew. My brother and sister-in-law had their first child, a boy. I left the ranch for a week to fly to Philadelphia and welcome the new member of our family. I cried the whole time.

The baby was a blessing. Our family was expanding. But all I felt was the absence of two people who should have been there to greet him, too. When I saw my nephew's face for the first time, I got scared. First of all, he looked like Mr. Magoo—bald and wrinkly. Then, when I held him, I saw my father's eyes and also his chin. And wasn't that the Nuddle thumb? I hadn't seen my parents in years. I'd forgotten what that *felt* like. And somehow, when I looked at this baby, I felt their presence. I didn't think I'd ever be able to look at my nephew without crying.

I couldn't be the only one having these feelings. I needed my brother to tell me what it felt like to have a child without my parents. I wanted him to tell me that the pain wasn't that bad. And if it *was* that bad, I wanted to hear that, too.

The week I went to Philadelphia, I stayed at my friend's house. There was too much commotion at my brother's and I wasn't feeling much like part of their new family, anyway. Three days before the *Bris* (circumcision), the phone rang. It was my brother.

"I want to talk to you," he said.

Oh good. He's finally going to tell me what all of this feels like for him. How he's hurting, but he's surviving. And I shouldn't worry because, when my time comes to start a family, I will too.

Instead, my brother said, "I want to give you your *Bris* lecture. When you come on Sunday, number one: do not use the ceramic cups from our cabinets for your coffee. You are to use Styrofoam cups just like everybody else. Number two: after the circumcision, Seth will be brought upstairs and you are not allowed to sneak any of Mommy's friends up to see the baby. I don't want to hear, 'It's only Flossie.' *No one* is to go upstairs."

"Are you kidding?" I asked, remembering how anal-retentive my brother can be about his home. But this was even more insane than his usual "Don't use the guest towel" lecture. My brother must have been in some real pain to obsess this much.

"Number three," he continued. "*You* can park your car in our driveway. But if you arrive with anyone else, *they* have to park in the street. That way, if we need something, you can be the one to go out and get it."

I was stunned. And yet, I should have seen this coming. It wasn't the first time that my fantasy of having a brother who'd sit around the kitchen table and talk about his feelings went down the toilet. In the five years since my parents' death, there had been a void. Not only had I lost my parents, I couldn't find my older brother. I seriously wanted to talk with the guy with whom I played Ping-Pong in the basement; the guy who woke me in the middle of the night to come along with his poker buddies to South Philly to have cheesesteaks before making our 8 o'clock classes.

When I was a younger, I honestly felt sorry for girls who didn't have an older brother like mine. I wanted *that* brother. Instead, I got a man who kept asking me when I was going to get a real job, or begged me to be sure to replace the pillows in the guest bedroom in their proper size order whenever I stayed at his house.

When we were growing up, my parents always said, "Be nice to each other. After we're gone, you are all you two have." But the distance between us kept getting bigger, and not because my brother had a wife and a family and I didn't. It was because with each passing year, more of our feelings were left unspoken. My brother didn't talk about my parents. Not to me, anyway. I'd hear from Seth's nanny how he'd pull out photos of my parents or talk about them to my sister-in-law.

One year, after searching his basement for boxes of family photographs, I asked him, "Don't you ever want to talk about it? Them? It? The whole thing?"

"O.K.," he said. "The next time you come over, I swear. We'll sit around for three hours and do nothing but get depressed."

I'm happy to say, things have gotten better between the two of us. It seems that having a son made my brother want to have his sister again. Who else besides me carried our family lore? One night, my brother called to ask me if I remembered the words to "A Capital Ship"—a song my father sang to us at bedtime.

"Oh, a capital ship for an ocean trip was the walloping window blind," I sang. "No wind that blew dismayed her crew or troubled the captain's mind. The man at the wheel was made to feel contempt for the wildest blow–ow–ow! Tho' it oft appeared when the gale had cleared that he'd been in his bunk below. So blow, ye winds, heigh-ho . . ."

"How the hell do you remember all that?" my brother asked.

"I remember," I said, "a lot."

Soon, my brother started calling me to let me hear Seth breathe or giggle into the phone. Or when Seth could sing all the words to the theme from *Gilligan's Island*. By then, I had met Oliver and we were becoming serious. And getting married definitely helped my relationship with my brother. In his eyes, I was becoming normal. My brother insists I got more relaxed. I think *he's* the one who relaxed. Either way, we felt safe enough to remember—together.

While Seth was a baby, I had dreams about him rolling around the floor of my apartment, crawling onto my stomach, and staring into my face. I felt the strong, unconditional love of a child. I thought, then, that it might be a wake-up call. Wake up and have a baby!

For months after my visits, I'd think about what it'd be like to have a baby of my own. Whenever I was alone in my apartment, I pretended I was pregnant. I'd get in and out of chairs, sticking out my belly, supporting my back with one hand as if I was in my seventh month.

Now, none of that feels possible.

Dream On

The stress of infertility is getting to Oliver, too. The other day, we woke up to find our car vandalized. Someone had stolen the turn signals and the side reflectors. Oliver was furious. Apparently, our 12-year-old Honda is worth much more in parts than if we sold the whole car. We've recently been shopping for a new car knowing that, when I got pregnant, we'd definitely want to have a car with dual air bags. But months have gone by, I'm not even close to being pregnant, and we still have the same old car.

The morning we went to file a police report, Oliver got into a fight with the desk clerk at the 24th Precinct. She didn't get off a personal phone call to take down his information and he was tired of waiting. He called two officers over and asked them if they could ask this woman to get off the phone. They wouldn't. Then Oliver stormed around the room searching for the Precinct supervisor. He looked crazed. He looked like I usually do at the check-out counter if the cashier is talking to her boyfriend at the next register instead of ringing up my order. "Relax," Oliver would say, as I would stare wide-eyed at her and then look around to get other customers to side with me.

I had never seen this side of Oliver.

"Don't you think I should find someone to *make* her get off the phone?" he asked me, desperately.

"Go right ahead," I told him. He needed to vent. Let him. I just hoped we didn't need the police for a real emergency. I told Oliver I'd wait in the car.

I didn't mind waiting. It would give me a chance to think about the dream I had the night before. I was in Seattle, visiting Ben Nussbaum. He was cuter than I remembered when I used to sit next to him in Hebrew School when I was nine. In the dream, I imagined he'd become a commercial artist who lived in a great apartment with high ceilings with large paintings on the walls. When I visited him, we sat on his bed to talk and, for some reason, he began to undress me and told me that he wanted to marry me. He leaned over to kiss me. It felt surprisingly good. Warm, exciting, I was floating. Then his girlfriend walked into the room. She was *pregnant*! So, of course, I told him I would *not* marry him.

For all the time I knew Ben, I never thought of him in a sexual way. First of all, he was short. I don't mean short for a kid. I mean he was a little guy. He was also kind of geeky. He was the one in my math class that wore his calculator attached to his belt. Years later, my mother told me she heard that Ben had gotten married and moved to Israel. By now, he was probably farming on a kibbutz with his three earthy, peace-loving children. Mazel Tov!

I didn't understand how I pulled Ben N. out of the Rolodex of my unconscious; although, ironically, there was another Ben N. that I dated my first year in college.

Trying

This one was gorgeous—tall, dark, curly hair, green eyes, good smile, great laugh. One day, my mother's friend, Eleanor, saw a photo of him on my desk and said, "I wouldn't care what there was to talk about. With that face, he's worth waking up to in the morning." As if I *was* sleeping with him.

"The point of all your dreams," my therapist explained, "is that you are remembering a time when infertility wasn't an issue. A time in your life when love and sex and making a baby were all very real possibilities."

I was dreaming of a *time gone by*? That hurt. And the pain was way beyond the emptiness I felt when I realized midriff sweaters and low-rise ripped jeans no longer felt appropriate for someone my age. Or when the woman at the makeup counter insisted on showing me an age reduction crème before applying any new foundations to my fine-lined skin. My therapist's words, while good-intentioned, made me feel even older. I saw the door closing on my fertility, and I tried, with all my might, to pry it open.

My friend, Mary, is pregnant. Three months. That means she had to have been pregnant at our last Christmas lunch. And she drank the champagne. Not fair. This will be her second child. Of course, I am happy for her. But I can't help but feel there is a wall that is growing thicker and thicker that separates what I am able to experience in my life from the things I can only witness in others. Her baby is due in August. I pray I'll be pregnant by then.

We got a letter this week from the Dr. Repeats-Your-Name-Too-Many-Times' IVF program. We've been "tentatively scheduled" for an IVF in April, depending on how well I score on my FSH test. I should prepare to come into the office on day three of my next period. Oliver and I never expected to hear from them again after the scheduling fiasco we suffered through last December. We suspected that their "tentative" approval was simply their way of saying they'd tried all they could for us. I checked my calendar. My appointment with the New Jersey doctors who perform cytoplasmic transfers came first. If their program takes me, I won't need the IVF in April and I'll get to tell them so.

All month, I've been religiously drinking my Chinese tea. I've increased my yoga practice to twice a week, have regular sessions with a chiropractor specializing in "womb harmonizing" adjustments, and swallow fistfuls of vitamins. I also signed up for "An Introduction to the Talmud" (Jewish Law) class for Oliver and me at the Jewish Y.

In Judaism, to study is to do a good deed. More than ever, the timing seems right, especially since I'd recently confessed to Oliver that I was starting to believe our interfaith marriage might be the cause of our infertility.

"I was waiting for that," he said, nonchalantly.

Trying

In truth, Oliver is innocent. From the very beginning, he was respectful of my religious observance and interested in attending Friday night services with me. When our relationship got serious, he signed us up for an interfaith counseling workshop so we could learn how to create a Jewish home while respecting his own religious background. I remember calling my girlfriend, with tears in my eyes, to tell her, "He signed us up for the course!" She, too, was in an interfaith marriage and knew which course I meant. It felt like Oliver had proposed!

Our first class in Jewish Law addressed those laws pertaining to divorce. For instance, if a spouse had lied about a previous condition that made it impossible to live with him or her—such as being a compulsive gambler or a drug abuser—the marriage could be ended. Or, if the man (or woman) had been hiding a physical deformity that the spouse found unbearable to live with, a Jewish divorce would be granted.

"Finally," the rabbi said, pounding his fist on the table as he spoke, "if the woman is unable to give her husband children, infertility is absolutely grounds for divorce!"

Well, I guess Oliver has just been given a permission slip from a higher authority to leave me. Then again, he's not Jewish. The laws don't apply.

For the first few weeks of our class, I was afraid to even stand near the rabbi. I was certain he'd pull me aside to say, "Barbara, you left the tribe. Why?"

During his lectures, I kept staring at him. Or rather,

he kept staring at me. He was trying to send me a message. *Leave him, my child, and you shall conceive.* But by the fourth week, I was so bored by learning the proper garb to slay a goat that I gave up trying to read his mind and worried more about staying awake.

Three days before our consultation for cytoplasmic transfer, the nurse called. She needed us to send our medical records immediately so the doctor could go over them beforehand. The night before our appointment, there was a message on our answering machine. "I'm sorry to tell this to your machine and not to you but your numbers are too high." Oliver looked at me in amazement. She never asked us about my FSH during our introductory phone call.

"I'm *so* sorry to have to leave this message on your machine," she repeated. "But I don't want you coming all the way out here for nothing."

For a month, I had stared at March 9 in my calendar as the day we'd be given a possible solution to all this hell. When Oliver spoke with the nurse the next morning, she explained that their program was for women who had difficulty with "embryo implantation"—not for women whose FSH was the problem. They didn't consider accepting patients with even slightly elevated FSH levels. Oh. How is it that this was never made clear to us? She did, however, offer up a name of another doctor in Manhattan to whom she'd referred other women like me. This doctor apparently treated each patient as an individual rather than a number and might be willing to consider me.

The second call from a nurse that week came from Nurse Alice from Dr. Repeats-Your-Name-Too-Many-Times' practice reminding me to come in for my FSH test. But by now, I've had my FSH tested enough times to know my levels will never be low enough for them. Instead of returning her call, I took a deep breath, sat down, and wrote the doctors in the practice a nice letter personally thanking them for all their help and concern. For now, I told them, we had begun to investigate "other options." I didn't want to say "other IVF programs" or even adoption. I just wanted to spare myself any further humiliation. Then I picked up the phone and called our next, best hope. They can't even see me until June.

The Show Must Go On

In the spirit of not letting infertility run our lives, Oliver and I decided to throw a huge party the night of the Oscars. We made all our guests get dressed as if they were actually going to the Academy Awards ceremony. Oliver wore a tuxedo. I wore a long, black evening gown. We had a red carpet running from the elevator to our front door, where Oliver stood with a clipboard behind a velvet rope. The hall was lined with life-sized drawings of spectators fighting to catch a glimpse of their favorite celebrities. As the guests entered, they were greeted by the flash of a camera, the glare of photofloods, and two life-sized golden Oscars set up on either side of the television.

For at least one night, Oliver and I thought about nothing more than making sure everyone had enough food, enough wine, and a pencil for the Oscar pool. As it turned out, both of the winners were two friends of mine from the gym—Gabe and Jeffrey. It was days before I saw them there to announce their good fortune.

"Guess what?" I said, walking over to Gabe who was pedaling away on a Lifecycle.

"Oh, my God!" he said, staring at me as he suddenly stopped pedaling.

"No, not *that*," I said, realizing he thought I was going to tell him I was pregnant. "You won the Oscar pool. So did Jeff."

"Great," he said, a little less excitedly. Then Jeff walked in. Before I had a chance to say anything, Gabe yells, "Barbara has something to tell you and I want to see your face."

"Really?" Jeff said, looking strangely at me.

"No, not *that*, I said, still trying to keep a smile. "You won seven dollars." I could tell he'd rather the other be true.

The same thing happened when we told my brother that Oliver was starting a new job. We called him to say we had some good news. David yelled, "Jill, pick up the phone! Pick up the phone!" As we told them about

Oliver's new position, I could tell they were a little disappointed. There was a void in my heart when we hung up. I decided I had to stop using the phrase, "I have good news."

People keep asking me how I am and I say, "Great!" And they say, "Really? Why?" Then I say, "No." And then I'm not having a great day anymore.

The gym has always been my refuge. Three times a week for over 10 years, I know exactly who will be there and when. One of the trainers is pregnant. She is there every time I go. It's hard watching her belly grow every week; watching her wardrobe change while my stomach stays flat. I wonder if she knows I'm trying. I wonder if she thinks I'm doing something wrong. I try not to stare at her, but every once in a while, Gabe or Jeff will yell, "Wake up, Barbara!" and I'm sure that they have caught me.

I decided to take a break from all treatments. Chinese medicine works more subtly than the Fertinex injections, however it has been weeks since I stopped sipping on tree bark and my ovaries still ache. I deserve a break. I need a break. But, I *feel* like I'm not trying enough.

While my body recovers, Oliver and I agreed to at least investigate the egg donor program my gynecologist had recommended. We felt we had to. There's a certain story that seems to travel in fertility circles that goes like this: "You know the Snyders? Marc and Lisa? Well, they were trying for *years*! They had just signed the adoption papers and, guess what?"

For me, signing up for egg donation was the same. Maybe then, God would see how serious I was about becoming a mother and reward me with a child of my own.

The introductory seminar was a three-hour class, during which time they tell you about the process of egg donation: where they find the donors, how they are screened, and what steps to take if you're interested. I was nervous, but knew I could count on a cup of coffee waiting for me in the lounge. The pastries in the seminar room were a nice touch, too. Then the nurse in charge of the program walked in. Everyone could see that she was at least seven months pregnant. Are they nuts? Let's invite a group of infertile women to sit around and learn about a procedure that involves inserting another woman's eggs into their bodies and have a perky, young nurse in a black maternity dress and pearls be the teacher. Perfect.

Registering for the program involved taking a test—the MMPI, or Minnesota Multiphasic Personality Inventory. The test consists of 567 multiple-choice questions as well as 50 true-or-false ones.

"Don't worry," the nurse told us. "The test is designed to weed out only those people who have severe depression or personality disorders."

Well, let's see. I'm signing up to use someone else's

eggs to make a baby because mine may not be good enough. How do you *think* I'm feeling?

Two weeks later, Oliver and I sat in the doctor's waiting room, pencils in hand (he was required to take the test, too), and were handed a plain, brown manila envelope with the test inside. Once I got a look at the first few questions, I immediately pulled out a piece of paper and began taking notes on the ones I'd want to discuss with my therapist.

- *You feel anxiety all the time.* True.
- *Experience fitful sleep.* True.
- *More nervous than most.* True.
- *Wish you were dead.* Uh, I'll say false. But there are days.
- *Hear voices.* No. Thank God, there's somebody out there worse than me.
- *Usually expect to succeed.* False. Well, it'd look better if I say "true," but the truth is, lately, I'm feeling . . . False. I wonder what Oliver is putting down.
- *I like mechanics magazines.* False. An easy one.
- *I like dramatics.* True.
- *At times, I think I am no good at all.* True.
- *Often, I feel not as good as other people.* True. I'm sure Oliver put "false." I pray to God his answers will be more normal than mine and they'll view us as a balanced couple. Either that or they'll call

him up and say, "Your wife's nerves are shot. I suggest you find another partner."
- *Wake up fresh and rested.* They must be kidding. False.
- *I have little to do with my relatives now.* True. Not that I wouldn't like to. But after my parents died, we stopped having the traditional holiday gatherings. Nobody was willing to make the holiday meals because everybody's family lived in a different state and the ones in the same state weren't talking to each other. Ever since my Uncle Morton sold the glass business to his sons, there has been resentment and anger over the terms of the deal. Now they can't stand being in the same room together—even for the Jewish holidays. I was never really close to my extended family, anyway. It wasn't *my* fault. It had more to do with the relationship my parents had with their siblings . . . Oh, I'm sorry. This isn't an essay question, is it?

Passed Over

It is approaching the time of year when I need to clean the kitchen for Passover. I start by removing every shelf in the refrigerator and wiping them down with a hot rag, like my mother did. I throw out any bread or food that is considered not kosher. I do the same thing in my cabinets. Then I take out each and every dish and piece of silverware and run it through the dishwasher twice to make them kosher for Passover. God bless ritual!

I like the Jewish Holidays. They're a time to pull out my grandmother's silverware and my mother's sponge cake recipes. Seeing my mother's handwriting is, at first, a bit upsetting—then comforting. I haven't thought much about my mother lately, which I find hard to believe. The feeling is similar to when you finally stop mourning and get on with your life. Weeks go by and, suddenly, you catch yourself thinking, "Oh my God. I forgot to miss them." All the science surrounding infertility has blocked out thoughts of my mother. I don't want my mother to "see" what I'm going through. What would she say?

Well, first she would say, "Am I allowed to know what's causing all of this?" Then, "Is this really necessary? The drugs? The shots?" Or else she'd say, "Forgive me. I don't understand. Bernice Rosen's daughter had the same thing you have and she has twins already." Or worst of all, "Barbie, I am so, so sorry. What can I do?"

For the moment, I am glad she's not here.

At the Passover Seder, Jews around the world tell the story of the exodus—of leaving one place for another. We remember the story by eating certain foods and abstaining from anything that could be made into bread. Our rituals serve to prepare our bodies, which are like vessels, to receive enlightenment.

To complete the Passover cleaning ritual—which

doesn't *have* to extend into the bedroom but, for me, it usually does—I cleaned out my closet. I finally got rid of the "What If" collection. As in, what if I was invited to the Academy Awards on short notice? Wouldn't I need this gold lamé evening gown that I bought at a sample sale? Or, for those impromptu weekends in Vermont, wouldn't I need all the ski sweaters from my very first job in knitwear that I stored in boxes I forgot I had?

I've learned. I've been to ski resorts and wanted nothing to do with the clothes I'd been saving all those years. The clothing I gave away today had nothing to do with future fashion events, but it has everything to do with expectation. I gave away the clothes I had carefully saved, season after season, thinking I'd wear them when I got pregnant. I am tired of moving my oversized T-shirt dresses from storage trunk to hangers wondering "Will this be the season?"

I wasn't giving up. I was only giving up torturing myself for not getting pregnant. For years, I hung on to these sacred fashions thinking that, when I *did* get pregnant, it would be fun taking a trip down memory lane. As if I'd want to wear the batwing T-shirt dress from the early 80s that reminds me of my old boss! Instead, I decided to start spending my time fantasizing about which one of my fashion friends would create my designer maternity collection. I will shop. I might even pay retail. And I will feel victorious! Just don't let me be in my ninth month during the summer. I'd still prefer my heaviest months to be during sweater season.

Passover in Philadelphia was what I expected. There was the usual crew around my brother's table plus a separate table for everyone's children. I'd grown accustomed to the faces I'd see around the Seder table. They were my brother's carefully selected new family.

The first year my brother decided to make the Seder, he decided you were invited only if you'd experienced a tragedy in your family. By then, my cousin Alan had stopped talking to his father. My brother's friends, Michael and Marsha, had lost their parents from illness in recent years. Same thing for the Cohens. One couple still *had* their parents, thank God. But she wasn't Jewish and his family wasn't religious. They were happy to have somewhere to go.

It never bothered me to spend every holiday with my brother's married friends and their children. For the most part, I was happy to be free and single in New York while celebrating their expanding families. Now, I notice that the kids' table is getting even bigger as the strollers disappear. The children walk. They talk. They've learned to read their own bedtime stories. And all I want to say is, "STOP! Could everyone please just stop while I'm trying to conceive? Everyone may continue growing once *I* have a baby."

Every year, after synagogue, my brother, sister-in-law

and the kids have lunch with my aunt and her two children. It's always a challenge trying to fit in a lunch between the end of services and the second night's Seder. But my family is divided. The only way to see everyone is for Oliver and me to run from house to house. And you can't have a visit without a meal. The whole holiday becomes "get in the car, eat; get in the car, eat; get in the car, eat."

This year, to save time, we met at a restaurant near the synagogue. There was much discussion over why they didn't have fruit salad on the menu. "Isn't this a kosher deli? Don't they realize it's Passover and that, after all the matzah, we *need* fruit?"

Dinner was only an hour-and-a-half away. We settled on some more matzah and butter. There was talk of how much my nephew has grown. He told us a joke. We laughed and applauded. Then we listened to my niece say her name. My cousins learned that I was trying and that the trying had become difficult. That is all I said. I didn't want to get into a whole explanation. It was Passover. I felt empty enough.

"Have you tried taking drugs?" my cousin asked. "My girlfriend took a drug—I don't know what—and got pregnant, right away.

"Yes, I have been taking drugs. It's a long process, but we're hopeful," I said, wanting to end this conversation and move on to the next subject.

"You know, I have a friend who sells her eggs to make money," she continued.

"Really?" I said, watching the matzah I'd been holding crumble under the pressure of the butter and my knife. "You know, I've heard of that."

"She's a bartender and a lounge singer and she sells them *all the time.*"

I pictured the mother of my child setting up shots of Wild Turkey at some bar in upstate Pennsylvania just before they call her up to the make-shift stage to do a set of Bonnie Raitt's greatest hits.

"She gets these shots in her arm that help her produce more eggs," my cousin added, wanting to sound informed.

"I have to take those same drugs," I said, trying to let her know that I understood a little more than she thought I did. "And I can assure you, she's not getting those shots in her arm."

The Car That Sells Itself

I cannot ingest one more thing. My kitchen counter is lined with potions, prescriptions and vitamins to treat something that I am tired of thinking about. I wish I could quiet all the voices in my head. Take it all! Read it all! Be prepared! Watch what you eat! Keep yourself fit! Relax! Be positive! Oh, get real. Despite all the stories

I've read about "miracle" babies, I don't think I'll ever get pregnant on my own. At the same time, I wish all the more that I could.

What fun that surprise would be! I'd get to greet Oliver at the door with my newly glowing face and coy smile. "Guess what?" I'd say in that nauseating tone I've seen in too many commercials. "We're having a baby." Oh, how I wish we could have a "guess what." Our marriage needs a "guess what." So much of our married life has revolved around planned sex and ultimate disappointment. What a thrill a surprise would be. Oliver and I would have celebration sex and, afterward, I'd get to keep my legs down.

Instead, we bought a car. Actually, we leased a car. We weren't sure what to do. We wanted to feel like it was ours. Before we decided, we had driven out to our friends, Brad and Cimone, to see their new home in the suburbs. Oliver and I arrived while it was still light outside so their oldest son could show us how he learned to ride a big boy bike. Then their three-year-old came down the driveway in his tricycle. As we drove to the restaurant in their newly leased car, we kept asking, "When you first got the car—even though you didn't buy it—did you feel like it was yours? Does it feel like yours now? Do you have any regrets?"

The next day we went looking for a new car—a black Honda.

"I think I should tell you," our salesman said. "There

Trying

are no black Hondas available anywhere near New York City. In fact, there's a wait-list."

"What?" Oliver asked, in disbelief. "How long is the list? You know what? Never mind." And we walked out of the dealership.

We didn't want to hear about wait-lists. We didn't want to hear about other people wanting the same thing that we do. We wanted a car and we wanted it now. When we got home, Oliver sat on the phone and called every Honda dealership in the tri-state area. He found our car. We decided to lease. It felt like ours. Who the hell knows? If I absolutely had to, maybe I could adopt.

In the category of hedging my bets, we just completed phase two of the egg donor process. We met with a psychologist who went over the results from our psychological examinations. Apparently, I was normal. High strung, but normal. As I suspected, Oliver was the calm one.

"Have either of you ever been in therapy?" the psychologist asked when we first sat down.

"Although," she said wryly, "the question for my Jewish patients really should be, 'How *long* have you been in therapy?' She laughed, and admitted she can be quite the crazy Jewish mother. I assumed it was her way of letting me know she was a member of the tribe and had her own share of therapy.

She asked us how long we'd known each other and

how we met. The same type of questions my rabbi asked us before she agreed to perform our wedding ceremony. I told her a few of my best stories. Everyone laughed. I wanted her to like me. I wanted her to know me. If Oliver and I had to do this, I wanted her to help us find someone just like me, and I told her so.

"That's normal," she said. "Especially for someone as young as yourself. But you shouldn't get too hung up on characteristics. We all have a desire to see ourselves in our children. And if you use a donor, you're actually giving your child a head-start in not looking for yourself in him or her." She explained that the tendency to be a narcissistic parent is much less with parents who adopt or use a donor.

"It's much healthier!" she said, reclining a bit in her swivel chair. "Besides, by the time you're ready for your next child, you'll be able to clone yourself!"

Excuse me? Cloning? The *next* time I do this? Houston, we have a problem! I was so not doing *that*.

Before we left, she mentioned that Oliver had a great voice.

"I'm not surprised you fell in love with him because women often get attracted to a man by the sound of his voice."

Oliver and I laughed because I used to make fun of his voice. When I first met him, I called it his "radio voice." It felt good to be reminded of our early times together. It feels like a hundred years ago.

Hair Story

To keep myself feeling young, I've been doing more and more yoga. Whenever I do a perfect "Downward-Facing Dog," I feel virtuous. Until today, when I spent the entire class thinking about my hair. The class began innocently enough. Our instructor had us doing the "Child's Pose." That was exactly what I needed—to be nice to my inner child. Next, I elongated my torso and leaned over into the "Triangle Pose." That was when I broke the first rule of Iyengar Yoga: I looked in the mirror. My hair looked great. I'd recently started blow-drying my hair again and I looked much better with a softer style. Why didn't I do this sooner? Perhaps my hairstyle is related to my infertility.

When I was 25, after years of blow-drying my hair in high school and college, I decided, "No more!" I wanted to embrace the humidity, not hide from it. Curly hair was good, natural, freeing. It was the eighties. Ringlets were in. But not according to my mother. Upon picking me up from the train, she took one look at my hair and said, "You didn't have to rush. You could have taken a later train."

"No, this is it," I told her. I *thought* I looked good in those days. But did I really? I might have met someone sooner in straighter hair. Gotten married and . . .

"Bar–bara." Suddenly, I heard the voice of my instructor pulling me back into yogi awareness. "Let loose in the shoulders. Let loose. Let loose." She's onto me. She knows I'm lost in impure thoughts.

It was only after I got engaged that I fell in love with a hairstyle that required blow-drying. Maybe if I'd returned to the blow dryer sooner, I might have met different men—the right kind of men. Not the kind that taught me how to roll my own cigarettes or had the mappings of a cemetery tattooed on their chest.

I want to forgive myself; for the bad hair, the bad dates, the bad timing, the bad eggs. Then I noticed that everyone in the room was facing east and I was still stuck in the west, facing the mirror.

Be at peace with your body, I tell myself as I open my arms to take in a cleansing breath. I need to clear a pathway for my eggs, but I can't stop looking in the mirror. Ever since I've rediscovered the look of my teenage years (when my hair was straight), I realize how much I've missed that girl.

When I was first dealing with the loss of my family, I didn't want to look anything like the girl I was when I shared a bathroom with my brother. The girl with the Farrah Fawcett cut. The girl who blow-dried her mother's hair on Saturday nights.

"P–l–e–a–s–e! Do my hair," my mother begged. "I don't know how to do it like you do!"

I didn't mind. It's not like I had anything better to do. Back then, I was Cinderella waiting for my Prince Charming—preferably someone who didn't go to my high school because the guys there were all idiots. I'd wait. Back then, I believed anything was possible.

"Pull your tailbone down," my yoga instructor reminded us. "Let your abdomen get loose. RELAX your abdomen," she repeated to the class. But she's standing beside *me* placing her hand on my back while she speaks. I try desperately to let go. I exhale slowly, feeling my middle soften. Gradually, I turn my head to catch a final glimpse in the mirror. I watch my reasonably flat stomach become a small, relaxed bulge and wish for the day when I'll see a belly that is round and big and swollen.

The Birthday Party

My niece is turning two. I'm already starting to say things like, "How old is Remi? Let's see. We got married in '96, the same year Remi was born," which makes me sound like an old person.

Oliver and I are going back to Philadelphia for her party. I'm excited. I've done my homework. As my therapist suggested, and as I read in the *Resolve* newsletter (an organization for couples experiencing infertility), I've prepared myself for what I might be feeling at a child's party. The column was actually written in anticipation of Mother's Day and offered advice to infertile couples about dealing with family-oriented events. Ironically, prior to Mother's Day, I wasn't even thinking about anything sad. It was only after I read this column that I thought, "Oh my God, I don't have my mother and I *still* haven't become one." To celebrate our moms, Oliver and I chose to take a long ride upstate in our new car.

The birthday party was a week later. My brother's backyard was filled with two-year-olds and their parents who complained about how many other parties they had to bring their kids to that weekend. When those who knew nothing about my situation asked me, "When is it going to be *your* turn?" I said, "Thinking about it." For those who had seen me at Passover and wanted to know how the trying was going, I just smiled and said, "It's going."

"How do you stay so thin?" my aunt asks me *every* time she sees me. Surely she understands that staying thin is not my problem. But to her, I'm thin. All must be well. That's O.K. I guess I'd rather be thin and not pregnant than overweight and not pregnant. I grabbed a slice of pizza and circulated.

Before long, some people began to gather on the deck. Heather, from "Music Together," had arrived. I knew all about "Music Together." Oliver and I went with my niece to her Saturday morning class the last time we were in town. I knew the school bus song. I had my favorite instrument. And I knew all about the colored scarves you sway in the air as you dance. Now, my niece was all smiles as she stood in the front row at her party. My nephew and I were dancing. I was singing, too.

After a few numbers, I noticed my cousin and his

wife on the other end of the porch. I put down my tambourine and walked over to greet them.

"Ellen's pregnant," he says, before even saying "Hello." She just stood there smiling and nodding her head. Thank God for sunglasses. Was I not just in a restaurant with these people on Passover describing how much trouble I was having to conceive?

"Congratulations! How far along?" I asked. I kept my mouth moving, hoping words would keep coming out.

"We *just* found out. Almost six weeks."

"And you're telling people?" I was too stunned to edit myself.

"We're confident."

Oliver was standing right next to me and knew exactly what was in my head. *People are unbelievable.* Why do I keep expecting them to make room for *my* feelings? My cousin picked up a big bowl of M&Ms from the table. She refused. "No more M&Ms" she tells him. "They have caffeine in them." He puts the bowl down, smiling.

I'm breathless and I'm angry. There's a pain in my chest that I didn't expect to feel that day. I had mentally prepared myself for being around 20 children and their doting parents, but not for this. Oliver picks up the bowl of M&Ms and offers them to me. I downed a handful and returned to my niece and nephew who were now dancing in a circle. I hoped that by the time the song was over, my tears would dry. *You do the hokey pokey and you turn yourself around. That's what it's all about.*

Chapter Five

Summer in the City

The days are getting longer. Now I have even more time in the light of day to wait for something to happen to my body. I'm reading a new book about infertility. My eyes rapidly scan the pages looking for similarities between the author and me—a high FSH, older than 35, being turned away by her doctors. I wanted to see how this woman got her baby. As I suspected, there was *more* I could be doing.

In her book, she talks about the merits of drinking wheatgrass juice. I vowed to go to the health food store to try a shot just as soon as I finished the book, which I read in one sitting.

You see, Billy, Oliver will tell our future child. *We tried many things and then, one day, Mommy read something in one of her books about wheat grass juice. She drank it everyday for two months, and guess what? We got you!*

Once again, I found myself making up a story of how my baby will enter this world. When I was single, I'd sit at my desk after a great first date or maybe the first phone call and start to imagine a life with this person. I'd rehearse what we would tell our children about how Mommy and Daddy met and eventually married. These days, every unsuccessful month leaves me searching for a new scenario.

There was the time we turned our bed toward the river. Or the month I kept my legs up against the wall every morning for 20 minutes. Or the time we lit only red candles. Or the time we did nothing at all. With each passing month, you want to believe that *this* will be the month that your story begins—the one you'll tell your child about how they came to be.

Today, I drank my first dose of wheatgrass. Other than the fact that my breath smells like the inside of my father's lawnmower, it's not that bad. By now, I've swallowed a hell of a lot worse than this. And it was only an ounce, which I followed with a large carrot and apple juice. In the book, the woman did everything she could to get pregnant, including making a dramatic change in her diet. Eventually, her FSH level dropped and she got pregnant. I already eat like a child of Mother Earth—very little red meat, never anything fried, only whole grain breads. The only loophole was the wheatgrass issue. Now, I'm covered.

According to an article that was posted in my health food store next to the juicing counter, wheatgrass has been known to increase the fertility of cows in as little as two months. I have two months. When Oliver and I came back from my niece's birthday party, we agreed to stop the Chinese teas and resume chemical stimulation. It was day three of my cycle—one cycle away from my appointment with our newest doctor. I took a deep breath as I walked back into The Office of Reproductive Technology—the one I swore I would never go back to.

As the doctor (the nice one) inserted the sonogram wand inside of me, he casually asked me what other "options" I was exploring. I told him I had, in fact, registered for a donor program. He looked relieved. I did not mention the other IVF program we were about to explore. As long as he heard I was starting to accept that I might need, as he called them, "aggressive fertility measures," he was sympathetic and willing to help. He even told me, "A lot of people get pregnant while on waitlists," which made me feel even better. I wasn't beating a dead horse.

During my examination, he noticed I had a remaining egg from the previous month. Was this a remnant from the Chinese herbs? He gave me a blood test to see if the egg was producing hormones. It was, so that meant this was not a good month to stimulate. I'd have to wait until at least next month to try.

Well, Charlotte. One month the doctor couldn't give Mommy any medicine to help her make a baby. He told her she had to wait a whole other month. So, without any help from any herbs or drugs, we tried to make a baby all by ourselves. And guess what? We got you!

This month, I'm counting on just me and the miracles of wheatgrass. I've also given up ice cream. Bad timing since it's 85 degrees outside. The book said that I should eat only foods that "warm my womb." It's Memorial Day weekend and I'm loading my shopping cart with canned soup.

"And you know what else?" I told Oliver the other night while watching *him* devour a bag of Fritos. "I eat too much junk food!"

"You eat nothing!" Oliver said. "You are the healthiest person I know."

"Well, I never ate a Frito before *you, or* a potato chip!" I said, staring at his stomach, which, miraculously, was flat.

"So, you're saying this is MY fault?" he asked, while tipping the bag sideways for the remaining crumbs.

"Maybe."

I wanted Oliver to give up Fritos. It was about time he deprived himself of something.

Trying

* * *

The woman who wrote the book about conceiving against all odds also ran a support group. It was around the corner from my apartment so I decided to go. Everyone sat in a circle and we went around the room telling each other where we were in our struggle with infertility. There were women older than I am with a lower FSH who were turned down by IVF programs because of their age. There were women who just started the process but refused to take drugs. And there were women—plenty of them—who had been through even more heartbreaking experiences than I trying to conceive. Women who had IVFs followed by miscarriages. Women who had donor eggs followed by miscarriages. Women who were trying to get pregnant but didn't have the support of their husbands.

When it was my turn, I spoke about my FSH, and then I told them how I hated listening to doctors or friends who keep suggesting other ways for me to have a child. "For me," I said, now crying to a roomful of women I neither knew nor was sure I liked, "the pain isn't just related to my infertility—it's about losing my parents *and* being infertile. That's why I want to do everything I can to make a child of my own." Oy yoy yoy! I went on too long. As if naming my problem would make the problem go away. For God's sake, infertility is a loss for everyone, regardless of whether or not you have a mother.

But sometimes I think I deserve a child more than other women do. And other days, I think I'm lucky because my strength has already been tested. I know I can ultimately handle it if I'm never able to conceive my own child. Forget I said that, God. Don't test me again.

After listening to the other stories, I left the meeting feeling surprisingly good about myself. Despite my doubts, I'd been doing many things right.

The Absence of Chaos

Oliver and I just came back from a weekend at our friend's beach house where we spent hours listening to their nanny troubles.

"We had Samantha's birthday party all set and then, on the morning of the party, our nanny called in sick. We had to dress the baby, get to the bakery before it closed, *and* set the table for 16 kids—all between 3:00 and 5:00 in the afternoon!"

"What a week!" they said. "Not that we're complaining," they added, almost as an afterthought—as a nod to what this kind of complaining must sound like to us. "But, you know, life is tough."

"Yes, it is," I said, sick of hearing about their cancelled nanny for the third day in a row. "I feel exactly the same way when I'm injecting drugs into my thigh night after night."

Surprisingly, Oliver, who I was certain would give me a "why do you feel you have to compare yourself to *them*" look, chimed in. "Especially when I have to give Barbara the shot. I thought I'd be totally calm about it but let me tell you, it's very scary holding a needle in front of the butt of someone you love."

"Thank you," I mouthed to Oliver, grateful to see I could pass the baton. I love that man.

Later that night, I felt like my comments were beneath me. I didn't really want our close friends to have to edit themselves when they're with us. But this trip felt particularly difficult. Another holiday weekend spent at the Jersey shore where Oliver and I cheerfully accompany other people's kids to the amusement park. Another holiday spent taking them on the Tilt-a-Whirl because their parents refuse to go. Another opportunity to see people I haven't seen since leaving Philadelphia, except now they have their kids in tow. This year, I so wanted to be banned from rides with signs that read, "DO NOT GO ON THIS RIDE IF YOU ARE PREGNANT."

O.K. Our friends' nanny didn't show up one day. For them, that's chaos. But how would you like having to live with the unpredictability of infertility treatments for nearly three years? Trying to work around blood tests, injections, sonograms and inseminations that can't be scheduled. And what if you're hoping for an IVF? You wait, you wait, and wait some more for the next part of your life to begin. No, this isn't the type of chaos our friends experience. It's worse. Infertility is the absence of chaos. It's waiting, and it's crazy.

When I was in college in Philadelphia, I met a guy named Gary. He was the one good thing to come out of Marketing 101. Gary and I spent many afternoons after class sitting on the grass talking about our families, especially while my father was sick. I remember confiding in Gary that I was having a hard time dealing with my father's illness. He hadn't been the same since his first operation. I wasn't the same, either. It didn't feel like I loved him anymore.

"Barb," Gary said. "The trouble you're having is that you expect too much. What you need to do is renegotiate your expectations. Stop wanting him to be something he may not be able to be. Love him for who he is now. Your relationship will be better and your life will be better."

I keep repeating Gary's words in my mind. Back then, he was one of the first people I'd known who'd been through therapy. He even went through est—a two-weekend course designed to help you more fully experience life. I fell in love with him. One time, I brought him home to dinner. After he left, my mother said, "He's gay." I said, "It's only his New York accent." My mother turned out to be right.

Years later, Gary and I found ourselves together again, working in New York. He worked in a showroom in my building and we'd sit on the steps between our floors and resume our conversations about life. He was as fed up with the garment center as I was. One day, while running down Seventh Avenue trying to hail a taxi with a large bag of samples slung over my shoulder, I ran right into him. I looked at him and asked, "When does the happy part start?"

He took the bag off my shoulder and looked me right in the eyes and said, "Barb, this *is* the happy part."

Gary died on his thirtieth birthday from AIDS. I often think of him when I'm struggling to enjoy my life in the face of all my losses. Gary and I were the same age. I feel obligated to live the life he didn't get the chance to. I also think of my friends Sal or Steven or George—all the friends I've known who have had their lives cut short. I owe it to all of them to make the most of my life. They would tell me I owe it to myself.

Recently, my therapist told me about a study that found the stress women suffer from infertility—the uncertain diagnosis, prolonged treatments, the "yes or no" phone calls that determine our fate—is the same stress that people diagnosed with cancer or AIDS experience. I thought about Gary's words. Once again, I need to renegotiate my expectations.

Mr. Toad's Wild Ride

After my yoga class this week, my instructor, Adrienne,

and I walked to the community garden to see if they put the goldfish in the pond for the summer. I rarely go to the garden. I'm usually too busy hauling my groceries down 97th on the way to my apartment to remember that there's an urban oasis on the top of a neighboring building. But that day, I was present. That day, I wanted to go. Adrienne told me I seemed peaceful.

"And I know," she said, "it's been a hard year for you."

"True" I said, staring into the goldfish pond. "Things are not happening the way I planned—AGAIN." I laughed. Adrienne's known me for years. She knew what I meant. Having lost her mother when she was 16, she and I have had our share of bonding conversations.

"I'm finally getting it," I told her. "Things are happening to me in ways that are so remote from what I'd ever experienced. I'm finally learning to love the day-to-day. Lately, I just view my life as Mr. Toad's Wild Ride. It's been quite liberating."

To celebrate our two-year wedding anniversary, Oliver and I dined as the sun was setting at the Boathouse Café in Central Park, where we were married. We love the park. We both think of it as a place that kept us company when we were single, and a favorite destination as a couple. By getting married there, we knew we could always return to the spot where we exchanged our vows. Some weekends, we'll take a walk through Central Park just so we can have a hot dog at the concession stand and look out over the lake at Bethesda Fountain.

Oliver and I have spent our entire married life dealing with infertility. At times, we make love with a heavy heart, but we're not afraid to talk about it. In some ways, it has brought us closer. When we went to interfaith counseling before we got married, the teacher encouraged us to talk about our upbringings, our family values, and our views on religion—any religion. We found it to be a wonderful experience, one that any couple could benefit from even if the partners are of similar faiths. Infertility has forced us to focus on bigger issues. It's prompted conversations about marriage, about what it means to be a parent and, ultimately, what we think is important in raising a child. Some people never have those conversations.

The day after our anniversary, Oliver and I went to London for a few days. He had business there and we were thrilled to be traveling together again. We fell in love on a road trip to Maine four years ago. It took eight hours to drive home and, for eight hours, I stared at his profile as we talked and sang to the radio. By the time we were face to face again, we knew it was the beginning of something. Now, whenever I see Oliver's profile in any moving vehicle, it reminds me of how we began.

The last time I'd been to England was to visit a potter whom I had become friendly with at an artists' colony one summer. On that trip, my days were spent mostly in Derby, a town two hours north of London.

"You're going to Derby?" my old roommate exclaimed. "It's dark and wet and they have overcooked meat. You're gonna hate it!"

"Thanks, Carol. I'm leaving tomorrow."

"Well, get out of there as soon as you can! Are you in love? If you're in love, it won't matter. But if not . . ."

As she hung up the phone, I could still hear her laughing.

Unfortunately, the trip was neither romantic nor relaxing. She had failed to warn me about the heat. There is none. I had to decide an hour before taking a shower to go into the bathroom to put coins in a heater and wait. Perhaps if I had been in love, it wouldn't have mattered.

For the trip with Oliver, my expectations were, naturally, higher. And I was also better prepared. Mark, my "never travel without knowing where to shop" friend, provided me with a list of what he considered "must sees."

"They've redone the Gucci store. It's *genius*! You have to go," he pleaded. "And when you get to London, immediately buy the latest copy of *Wallpaper* (a London lifestyle magazine), check out the index, and go everywhere! There's a store in Covent Garden, Fresh, that sells the most amazing lip gloss."

Our first day, Oliver was working back at the hotel and I went, shopping list in hand, to Covent Garden. I immediately recognized a few places I'd been to years before. For a change, I took pleasure in remembering my past. Working my way across town, I realized I was happy to have had all these chapters, even if they did cut into my childbearing years. After a few hours shopping the stores, the pressure from seeking out the ultimate lip gloss was wearing me down. I removed myself from Sloane Street—the land of Harvey Nichols, Joseph, Gucci, etc.—and went to a gallery in the South End to see a sculpture exhibition.

I was transformed. I stood in a large room and looked straight ahead to what I thought was merely a blank, white wall. When I looked closer, I saw a white wall with a gray circle painted on it. As I moved from side to side, I suddenly realized that the circle wasn't painted but was created by a large, inverted dome carved into the wall. I stood in front of the dome and, wherever my eyes traveled, all I could see was white. I got lost in it. No matter how hard I focused, it seemed to get brighter.

Staring into the dome, I felt safe, enlightened, as if I was observing a kind of absolute truth. I may be overstating this piece of wall, but it had been a long time since I *felt* brightness. Its white glow had the familiarity of a shining sun, only brighter. It was a welcome contrast to the darkness I'd been confronting in the middle of the night.

I walked toward another wall and another installation and, again, saw nothing but what appeared to be a blank wall. However, this time, as I walked past the wall, I noticed it had a protrusion, which got bigger or smaller depending on where I stood. It made me think of pregnancy, and how it eludes me. At the end of the exhibition, I learned the title of the piece. It was called, "When I am pregnant." I considered this a sign.

For our last day, Oliver and I took a field trip to the outskirts of London to Hampstead, a beautiful suburb that features the homes of some great writers as well as the home of Sigmund Freud. After all my years in therapy, I had to get a look at *the* couch. I felt like I owned a piece of it. Afterwards, Oliver and I went into the village to a tiny Moroccan restaurant. We immersed ourselves in a huge platter of pita, hummus and olives. While we were having fun making each other little sandwiches, a woman entered and sat next to us. She was alone, seemed to be a regular, and as she ordered her glass of wine, she sounded as if she'd had a few before entering this establishment. I felt sad watching her so I leaned over and asked her if she was from the area. We all got to talking about the neighborhood, New York, and about her daughter who had lived in the States for a semester of college.

"Do you two have any children?" she asked.

"No," we both said, mid-bite, looking slightly uncomfortable. "We've only been married for two years," I quickly added, wanting her to think we were child-*free*, not child-*less*.

Her question frightened me. I envisioned Oliver and I five years from now in another foreign country drinking wine, touring the countryside, pretending to enjoy being just the two of us. Are we becoming the nice married couple who never had any children? No! That was my parent's generation. If we really wanted a child, we know there are many ways we could have one.

Still, I wonder at what point a couple makes peace with the idea of going through life without children. Would we spend another year trying to conceive on our own while searching for new technology? Would IVF even work? And if not, would we try again, use a donor, or think about adopting?

Years could go by and then, one day, we'd look at each other over dinner and say, "We're too old, we have other interests and we've made our lives full without raising a child." Will that really be what we want, or will we have become too exhausted to try anymore? To not be able to tell the difference would be a shame.

New Beginnings

The day after we came home from London, I got my period—four days early. Which meant that if I was going to go in for a "day 3" test with the new doctor, it would be sooner than I or they'd expected. I called his office to let them know I'd be coming in two days.

The office of Dr. M was smaller than the ones I've been to so far, but it still had the horseshoe of chairs around a square glass table, a water cooler, an assortment of monthly magazines, and the obligatory patient education pamphlets. Remarkably, this office only had two: one about female incontinence (at least *that* hasn't happened yet), and another about hormone replacement therapy. There was also a *Resolve* newsletter as well as business cards for the pharmacies in the area that carried fertility drugs.

As I leafed through *People* magazine's "Sexiest Man" issue, a woman came out of the door leading to the exam rooms followed by a nurse who asked me to come in. She led me directly to Dr. M's office, which caught me by surprise since I expected her to take my blood first. Usually you have to bring in the witch's broom before you get to see the Wizard.

Dr. M stood up to greet me. He was shorter than I'd imagined. That's fine. Maybe he didn't date a lot in medical school because of that, which might have made him a better student. He motioned for me to sit down.

"I've gone elsewhere," I confessed. "They tell me my FSH is too high for them. I was wondering . . ."

"Hold on . . ." he said, getting out a piece of paper and starting to write. I think I may have gotten a little too emotional too fast for him. He started jotting things down. Probably something like, "Patient appears manic." Then Dr. M. looked up with a fatherly expression and said, "Start from the beginning. Who told you what?"

For the next 10 minutes, I filled him in on my recent adventures. I left out the names of some of my doctors but he seemed to know who I was talking about—

especially Dr. Celebrity. He told me that he has helped women with elevated FSH levels (I loved that he said "elevated" and not "off the chart"), but that every case is different and the odds would not be in my favor. He also added that, because he was affiliated with a major teaching hospital in New York, there would still be a wait-list to contend with. He ended our discussion by saying he would consider accepting me into the program once he saw my latest lab results and reviewed my medical records. He walked me over to an exam room where a nurse was waiting for me with a needle. I was never so happy to be pricked.

The next day, my heart was racing when Dr. M's office called. The nurse told me that my numbers were borderline but acceptable, as long as they remained relatively stable for the next two months. Oh my God! "Acceptable?" I haven't heard *that* word used all year. I wanted to jump up and say, "Take me *now*. *Today*, please, before they get any higher." But it doesn't work that way. I have to wait.

Summer is in full swing now, and with the prospect of finally moving forward, I'm loving the extra hours of light. I get excited by picnics in the park, day trips to the beach, sleeping in the sun, strolling on wet sand, silently wondering if this will be our last summer as only two. Tonight, I gave myself a facial—the first in a very long time. It feels great to pamper myself again. But as the day winds down, I realize something about myself that has remained with me for as long as I can remember: I'm afraid of the darkness. A sad feeling often comes over me as a day comes to a close and you can no longer see outside. Even though I'm safe in a home that I love, making dinner for a man that I love, watching the dark, blue sky turn into the black of night still feels like a death to me. Even though I know that I'm more than ready to be somebody's mommy, there's still a part of me that will always feel like the little girl afraid of the dark—and of dying.

Everyday, I try to picture what my life will look like with a child in it. I try to feel what it will be like to stroll along with my baby. I'd finally get to wear one of those Baby Bjorn carriers that hold your baby on your chest. Since I'd be with the baby during most of the day, Oliver would probably insist on carrying the baby at night and on weekends. And, of course, I'd let him.

The other night, I was having drinks with two friends I used to work with when I was in the garment center. As we sat at an outdoor café in the West Village, I noticed a lot of couples passing by with babies.

"See *them*," I said, pointing to a well-dressed couple and their baby. "I can just imagine Oliver and I going out for dinner in the Village and then walking around with our Baby Bjorn."

"You're going to name your baby *Bjorn*?" one of my single friends asked.

Trying

It's satisfying to know that I still have friends who aren't so caught up in the baby game to know I was talking about a baby carrier. I love escaping my fertility worries by meeting my single friends. My married friends go out, too, but not as often. And when they reach for their wallets, they always seem to pull a pacifier from their pocket, like it's a Girl Scout badge. They wave it in the air and say, "See this? This is my life now!" Well, I have a few badges myself. One's for pain, the other's for suffering. But I choose to leave them home.

My goal right now is to act as normal as possible while praying for my life to change. Time has been crawling by. Movies help. Still, I can't sit through the length of a feature film without wondering if, one day, I'll be able to balance a bucket of popcorn on my protruding stomach.

My period came—finally. The process officially begins. I stared at the pinkish stain on the toilet tissue and thought about the very first time I saw something similar appear on my underwear. I remember taking them off and putting them in my top dresser drawer to show my mother when she got home. I don't remember if she said anything. It was awkward. We both kind of looked at each other, hugged, and went into her bathroom in search of a box of sanitary pads she'd been saving for me. That night at dinner, I remember my father tapping me on the arm, smiling, and then giving me the O.K. sign.

When I left the bathroom, I went over to the photo of my parents on my bookshelf and asked them to pray for me.

Day three. I went into the doctor's office and Veronica, a nurse I had never met before, gave me the blood test. Then Dr. M explained how my IVF would proceed. The fact that he was telling me all of this made me feel confident that it might actually happen. The plan was for them to interrupt my natural cycle and administer a drug called Lupron, which suppresses my body's own hormone production. This will require daily injections for the next two to three weeks and will ensure that my eggs don't ovulate prematurely. O.K.

About 10 days into the process, I'll begin taking other injections to stimulate my ovaries for egg production. It's all about creating a controlled environment to produce the highest number and highest quality eggs. Fine. Sounds good. During that time, they'll want me to come in regularly to test my blood and to give me an ultrasound to monitor the growth of the follicles. This last part sounded familiar because I had to be monitored each time I was stimulated prior to an insemination.

When enough eggs have matured—about a week after stimulation begins—Oliver will give me a shot of HCG and I'll be scheduled for an egg retrieval. This is the moment we've all been waiting for. I am so ready. I wish I could fast-forward to the day when they take my eggs, mix them with Oliver's sperm, put the embryos back in my body and we find out whether we're going to be parents.

Later that day, the nurse called. She said, "Hi, Barbara. This is Veronica from Dr. M's office. The doctor has you down for Lupron to be administered tonight and every night until you receive further instructions. We've already called in the prescription so you can . . ." I couldn't believe it. She was talking to me like any other patient. She had no idea what I went through to get to this point (how could she?), or how thrilled she was making me by giving me instructions about dosages and injections. I can do this! I can absolutely do this! I was so in my thoughts that I didn't notice she had stopped talking. I scrambled to think of something to say.

"Um. How soon 'til I need to come in?" I asked, not knowing she had just told me.

"We'll call you the day before, but it's usually about a week from the time you begin your injections. Call the office if you have any questions."

I didn't want this phone call to end. I hadn't felt this happy in months. I wanted to tell her that. I wanted to tell her everything. Instead, I simply said, "Thank you. Thank you so much," and hung up the phone to call Oliver.

"We're on!!" I said, laughing nervously. "This is it. This is the beginning! I can't believe it. Now I'm scared. What if it doesn't work?"

"You're unbelievable!" he said. "Can you just give me 10 seconds to get excited before you get nuts. Man!"

"You're right. I'm sorry."

"Did they tell you what your levels were?"

"No, I didn't ask. Should I have? What difference does it make? I'm starting. Now *you're* depressing *me*. Why do you always have to be so technical?"

"I don't know. I think a normal person, after going through what you've gone through, might ask."

"Well, I didn't. I'm sorry."

"No, I'm sorry."

"It's O.K. I'm going to go out now to walk down to the pharmacy, pick up my drugs and treat myself to an iced coffee—decaf."

"Great idea. I'll see you when I get home. I love you."

"I love you, too."

Whenever I see my Uncle Norman, he tells me that Oliver reminds him of my father. I know what he means. They have the same sense of responsibility, the calm demeanor, the voice of reason. But when Oliver and I fight, it's usually a struggle between wanting to make the other person happy and not losing ourselves. The fights often start with a seemingly innocent remark, then escalate to words meant to hurt, which can go on for quite awhile. And then, just as quickly as it started, the fight subsides when we realize how much we love each other. That was exactly the dynamic I had with my mother.

* * *

We told a few close friends that I'd be having an IVF "sometime in the late fall." I didn't want to tell them it was starting now and have everyone ask me how it was going. I was nervous enough. And even more importantly, if it worked, I'd get to surprise them with my good news just as if I'd gotten pregnant naturally. Say nothing. This was the gift I was giving myself.

There's one woman at my gym who continually asks me if I am pregnant. "So–o–o?" she asked this week as I lay next to her doing my sit-ups. "How's everything going?"

"Pretty good," I said, knowing this month could be the one.

"Are you pregnant?" she asked. She must have sensed my excitement.

I stopped my set of crunches to deliver the speech I have wanted to deliver to countless concerned observers.

"Please understand," I began, with the wisdom and nerve of two years of infertility behind me. "Even *if* I was pregnant, which I'm *not*, I wouldn't tell you. I wouldn't tell *anyone* until I was at least three or four months pregnant. So when I *am* pregnant, and when I feel ready, I will tell you. I *promise.*"

The Room for Waiting

I've become very cavalier about my injections. I often bring them with us when Oliver and I go out to dinner.

In between appetizers and entrees, I've been known to pull out my bottles and syringes inside a bathroom stall. As I wait for the alcohol on my leg to dry before giving myself the injection, I peer through the door and watch other women primping in front of the mirror. I can fill a syringe and inject it into my thigh in the same amount of time that other women apply lip liner.

I'm getting excited and also more anxious. I've now moved on to the stimulation phase, which means constant monitoring and twice as many drugs. I can't tell if my erratic behavior is the result of the stress or the drugs.

"I think the drugs are making me crazy," I told my friend, Victoria, the other day, during one of those, "how are you *really*" phone calls. "This morning at our local diner, I cried because my eggs were too cold."

"Really?" she asked. "Is that what they think is wrong with you?"

"No! My breakfast eggs," I said. "Not *my* eggs. Although, funny you should mention that because, all summer, I've only been eating foods that warm my womb."

I've been taking daily trips to the doctor where I've learned how to count the number of follicles that are growing and compare their size. As hard as I try to keep calm, my state of mind has not been helped by some of the women I meet in the waiting room. Today, two women kept telling me that the two weeks between the actual procedure and my pregnancy test will be hell.

"Do whatever you can to keep busy," they said, "even though it won't matter." They told me I won't be able to stop wondering if the strange feeling in my ovaries means "I am" or "I'm not."

Until now, I hadn't spoken much with the other women patients in any of the offices where I would wait—definitely not about anything more serious than where I got my watch and how hard it is to find one that looks good with gold and silver jewelry. But now that I was undergoing an IVF, not just a blood test or an insemination, I wanted to have a real conversation with someone about what I should expect. Big mistake.

"After my *first* IVF, I came in for my pregnancy test," one woman said. "It was positive. I was never so happy about vomiting!" I liked hearing that. I prayed for the day when I'd be legitimately nauseous.

"Then two weeks after that, I lost the baby," she added.

I decided, then and there, that if this works, I'm not going to let myself feel really happy until my kid's in the first grade.

"This is my second try," another woman said. "This is it. If it doesn't work this time, we're stopping."

I've heard of couples who go through IVF four or five times. If money was no object and the success rates were decent, why *wouldn't* they want to keep trying? Before I started any fertility treatments, I thought I'd keep trying, no matter what. But now that I haven't even completed my first IVF, I understand. Even if the results could result in having your very own baby, the injections and surgeries are mentally and physically draining, as is the waiting and the hoping. After a point, I can imagine that you just want your life back. And then there's the money.

This is the big league—seriously big. It's around $15,000 for each attempt, unless you're lucky enough to have eggs left over from a previous cycle. It's possible for them to freeze your eggs and you won't be charged for a retrieval. It's also possible to have embryos left over, which can be frozen and stored, too.

I pictured a future visit where a nurse might ask me, "Did you bring your own eggs? Embryos? Or will we be starting from scratch? *Will that be a cut and a color this week, or just a cut?*

To help kill time, I decided to go to the Museum of Modern Art to see a film. It was a Friday, and Oliver was able to end his day early to meet me. As I had planned, when I arrived at the museum, I opened up a membership figuring it will encourage me to visit more often in the months ahead. Maybe I'd even come back with my baby before the year was out.

The woman at the desk handed me my temporary membership card and two tickets to the movie. It was early, so I decided to peruse the Léger exhibition, whose entrance was right next to the theater where they were screening the film. A half-hour before the film started, I handed my ticket to the attendant.

"Sold out," she says.

"What do you mean, *sold out*?" I said, staring at the tickets in my hand.

"Just because you have a ticket doesn't mean you have a seat," she said, focusing her eyes on a clicker in her hand that registered attendance. "Sorry."

"And exactly how was I supposed to know this?" I said, my voice starting to quiver. My eyes began to fill up. I've waited. It was my turn. *What if I go through all this and my body doesn't produce enough eggs?*

"Are you sure there are no seats?" I asked. She didn't budge.

I went upstairs just as Oliver walked through the door.

"They're sold out!" I said, waving my tickets, starting to cry. Oliver looked totally confused. "They didn't tell me that having a ticket means NOTHING! I needed to go right in and now we're screwed."

As Oliver tried to understand my level of fury, I walked back over to the person who handed me the tickets and complained. She directed me to the Membership Services counter where a smartly-dressed woman in her late fifties nodded her head in empathy.

"I'd write a letter," she said, handing me a piece of paper. "It's disgusting." "Who do I address this to?"

"To the director of the museum."

Oliver watched me as I knelt on my hands and knees at the membership counter. It might have been the drugs, but there was no stopping my hand from scribbling my story on a piece of paper now wet from my tears.

"You're going to write this letter *now*?" Oliver asked, while looking at the woman as if she was the night nurse and I was a crazy psych patient.

"Yes I am."

"Don't you want to go home and think about what you want to say in a calm and concise manner?"

"I want to let the director know how I feel right at this moment," I said. "They need to understand my rage."

The minute I walked out of the museum, I felt really stupid for leaving that letter. I started to go back in and retrieve it, but Oliver insisted it would only make me look crazier.

I was warned about the side effects of the drugs I'm taking—insomnia, irritability, bloatedness, headaches, nausea. And now I'm afraid it's only a matter of time before I'll lose my grip on reality.

At a recent eye examination, my doctor asked me if anyone had mentioned that fertility drugs could trigger adverse effects. "For example," he said, "they can cause spontaneous blindness."

"Interesting. I'll keep that in mind," I said with no real enthusiasm, partly because my chin was stuck in a machine that measures my cornea and partly because I had stopped being concerned with the "adverse effect" section of prescription drug inserts. If I was truly concerned, I could never do any of this. But that wouldn't sound rational to a doctor whose toughest question to a woman may be whether she can read the bottom row of an eye chart.

Once my head was out of the cradle, I continued, "I like to believe my fertility doctors have considered the risks of these drugs. But, thanks. Now I have something else to worry about while my pupils are being dilated."

That was mean. I should apologize. He *is* my doctor. Fuck it. I don't have the strength.

I'm planning a surprise party for Oliver's fortieth birthday. He's been a bit edgy about turning 40 and I had so wanted us to have a baby in time for his birthday. Now I'm working on producing a pregnancy—or at least a fabulous party. The event is more than two months away, but I made all the invitations last week and have already addressed all the envelopes. I want to get this part done while I still have a shred of sanity. I'm not mailing the invitations until after the procedure. In the event that something goes wrong with the retrieval—like there aren't enough viable eggs or the implantation fails— Oliver and I might be so distraught that we'll want to do something drastic. Like leave the country.

On the other hand, what if the IVF works? I have no idea how pregnancy will make me feel. Will I get nauseous right away? Exhausted? Elated? Maybe I'll finally feel so excited that I won't be able to get any work done. God I hope so.

I've never felt more like my parents than I do planning this party. Getting married felt adult enough, but this business of turning 40 reminds me of being back in my old house listening to the laughter from the dinner parties my parents gave when one of their friends turned 40. Now, *I'm* the one changing the lyrics of show tunes, digging up old photographs and preparing the toasts. The party is being held at our friends' Susan and Jay's home in New Jersey because Oliver will never suspect anything in the suburbs. Susan is 44. So is Jay. They have a seven-year-old son. Susan was three months pregnant at her wedding. She wasn't concerned about being thin in her dress.

Your Eggs are Ready

After 11 days of stimulation, Dr. M seemed pleased by how well my eggs were maturing. Although I hadn't produced many eggs (which we expected, considering my age and FSH level), the quality of the ones I did produce was apparently good.

Last night at 10 o'clock, Oliver gave me my HCG shot—the one I'd already experienced twice before when I was stimulated. Thank God for the Food Network! This time, I found the land of slicing and dicing to be more soothing than watching furniture refinishing to distract myself from a three-inch needle. The retrieval is a day away.

As I looked out the window of the taxi on the way to the hospital, I felt very sentimental about places we passed—the bagel shop, the camera store, our local diner. We drove through the park and I looked around at all the paths I'd walked when I needed to be alone, yet with people. I love living in the city. I love the sidewalks for holding me up during many a mournful walk when I longed to go home to a home that no longer existed. This city saved me. "Thank God I had already moved out of Philly," I tell people who wonder what it was like for me those first few years after my parents death. "It's not like I have memories of me and my mom walking down Madison Avenue."

My parents only visited me a few times before they died, and those visits were strictly West Side. I still see my mother's face in places like Barney Greengrass, where she told the deli guy to "take care of my little princess." Or I remember my father standing by his car on West 73rd Street admiring his parking place the day they helped me move into my own apartment. They decided to use a taxi to move my few belongings so he wouldn't have to give up the space. But other than that, I rarely connect my parents to my life in New York City.

One of my first apartments was a tiny duplex I shared

with a would-be opera singer who had the habit of not announcing her "overnight" guests. I only learned we had company after stepping on a note she'd leave me at the top of the spiral staircase I had to climb on the way to the bathroom every morning.

Whenever my mother came to visit, she'd stare at the assortment of books, dusty stuffed animals and unidentifiable crafts and say, "I wouldn't worry about decorating. I would concentrate on removal." I slept on a pull-out sofa in the living room, a space so cluttered with my roommate's belongings I barely had room for my clothes and stereo. It wasn't until I moved into my own apartment—a junior one-bedroom that I would live in for the next 10 years—that I had to make decisions about furniture. And that was when my mother changed from the woman who took pride in saying "I have every confidence in your behavior" to some lunatic I'd never seen before.

My mother had come by train (without my father) and she was early, which wasn't a problem since it gave her time to look around the apartment while I finished getting dressed. My bedroom was separated from the living room only by a five-foot-high partition, which allowed me to watch my mother during her inspection.

"There's nothing wrong with *these* sofas" she said. "They're great!"

She was referring to the fact that my first sofa—the one we picked out together in Philadelphia—never made it into my apartment. The movers couldn't even fit it into the elevator because neither my mother, my saleswoman, nor I had thought to measure the sofa or my elevator. My mother *had* managed to find out that the son of our saleswoman also lived in New York, and she gave her my phone number to give to him.

After toying with the idea of having a futon, I ended up with a loveseat and sofa from Jennifer Convertibles. I later learned this combo was affectionately known by New Yorkers as the "subway collection" because, in the eighties, an advertisement for the pieces was prominently posted in every subway car. The grey-ish tweed, standard-sized pieces were nowhere near as exciting as the Italian-made, black, double-cushioned sofa that I really wanted. But, to use my mother's words, these "served a purpose."

I begged the store to sell me only one piece, but they insisted the two pieces were sold as a set. My friend, Mark had already made me buy a pair of club chairs because he told me that "when it comes to a good chair, nobody buys one." So, now in my new apartment, I owned two chairs, two sofas and a set of small, stackable glass cocktail tables a friend donated because he was redecorating. I had strategically placed the tables in the center of the room to look like one larger table.

My mother looked at the arrangement and said, "They're really perfect. But how come you have the tables over here? The loveseat should be much closer to the table so you can reach things. And why did you pick that wall for the sofa?

"Mom," I said. "I like it. I only have five pieces of furniture. Count them. Five. And you are trying to rearrange them."

As I walked back to my bedroom, I smiled. I knew that mothers like to impose their decorating taste on their daughters, but I was amazed she was capable of this with so few pieces to coordinate.

I remained calm, walked into my bathroom and started to run water for my contact lenses.

"The bigger sofa really should go over here, Barb," she yelled. Then I heard the sound of furniture scraping across my linoleum floor. I've never heard or seen her move anything.

"Mo–om!" I yelled, running out of the bathroom. "Do you mind?"

Staying calm was an effort, but I had to because I was holding a hard contact lens between my thumb and forefinger. Any display of anger could cost me 60 bucks to replace a cracked lens.

"Could you please sit down?" I begged. "I love you. Have some coffee. I'll come out in a minute and we'll discuss the furniture."

I started to laugh again—this time out loud. I was thrilled to have my mother's love and attention. But I'd assumed that my mother, the teacher—the woman with a master's in Psychology and Western Civilization—could control her urge to undermine my first attempt at nesting.

I returned to my running water. As I shut the door, I heard my mother mumbling to herself, "She's gonna kill me. But I'm just going to change this one sofa."

I raced from the bathroom. "I do NOT believe you!" I shrieked, my eyes barely able to focus as my mother hauled my sofa across the room.

"Why don't you have better lighting?" she asked. And then, "Aren't these floors awfully cold? Don't you *care* about carpeting?"

All I could think about was how hard I tried to create a space of my own, on my own. Other friends had their mother, along with their mother's credit card, decorate their entire apartments for them. I asked for nothing.

Then I did the unthinkable. I lunged at my mother. I had about two inches on her and was definitely stronger. I threw her onto the opposing loveseat. My God! How could I wrestle my own mother? Rage. Rage helps. Rage gives you the guts to throw your "means-well-only-wants-the-best-for-you" mother across a living room.

"Do you think I *like* doing all this myself?" I screamed while pushing my furniture back to its original position. "Don't you think I would prefer a larger cocktail table that balances the room? Of course I want carpeting!"

Then, in a moment of weakening, I said, "I'm alone,

Mom. I work hard. I have no time. I don't have Rent-A-Boyfriend to help me design and install track lighting. I don't ask you for money. I'm proud of what I've done. Of course it could be better."

My mother and I sat on opposite sides of the room panting from our rumble.

"I'm sorry," she said. "I had no idea you didn't want me involved."

A few moments passed. We were both emotionally and physically drained by the tug-of-war over my sofa. Our panting slowly became synchronized, eventually ending with a long sigh. We stared at each other cautiously.

"What time is it?" I asked.

"Twelve-thirty," she said.

"Great! Our reservation at Sarabeth's is for one o'clock. Are you ready?" I asked.

"Let's not take a cab," she replied. "I'm so excited to be here with you. Let's take our time and walk."

If you ask me what I miss most about not having my mother—I miss going to lunch.

When I pulled up to the door of the hospital, I suddenly felt giddy and tired at the same time. I hadn't slept well the night before. I had dreamed that I had given birth to a baby boy, but there was something wrong with his penis and he ended up in a trash can. I really need to stop watching the 11 o'clock news.

a master's in Psychology and Western Civilization—could control her urge to undermine my first attempt at nesting.

I returned to my running water. As I shut the door, I heard my mother mumbling to herself, "She's gonna kill me. But I'm just going to change this one sofa."

I raced from the bathroom. "I do NOT believe you!" I shrieked, my eyes barely able to focus as my mother hauled my sofa across the room.

"Why don't you have better lighting?" she asked. And then, "Aren't these floors awfully cold? Don't you *care* about carpeting?"

All I could think about was how hard I tried to create a space of my own, on my own. Other friends had their mother, along with their mother's credit card, decorate their entire apartments for them. I asked for nothing.

Then I did the unthinkable. I lunged at my mother. I had about two inches on her and was definitely stronger. I threw her onto the opposing loveseat. My God! How could I wrestle my own mother? Rage. Rage helps. Rage gives you the guts to throw your "means-well-only-wants-the-best-for-you" mother across a living room.

"Do you think I *like* doing all this myself?" I screamed while pushing my furniture back to its original position. "Don't you think I would prefer a larger cocktail table that balances the room? Of course I want carpeting!"

Then, in a moment of weakening, I said, "I'm alone,

Mom. I work hard. I have no time. I don't have Rent-A-Boyfriend to help me design and install track lighting. I don't ask you for money. I'm proud of what I've done. Of course it could be better."

My mother and I sat on opposite sides of the room panting from our rumble.

"I'm sorry," she said. "I had no idea you didn't want me involved."

A few moments passed. We were both emotionally and physically drained by the tug-of-war over my sofa. Our panting slowly became synchronized, eventually ending with a long sigh. We stared at each other cautiously.

"What time is it?" I asked.

"Twelve-thirty," she said.

"Great! Our reservation at Sarabeth's is for one o'clock. Are you ready?" I asked.

"Let's not take a cab," she replied. "I'm so excited to be here with you. Let's take our time and walk."

If you ask me what I miss most about not having my mother—I miss going to lunch.

When I pulled up to the door of the hospital, I suddenly felt giddy and tired at the same time. I hadn't slept well the night before. I had dreamed that I had given birth to a baby boy, but there was something wrong with his penis and he ended up in a trash can. I really need to stop watching the 11 o'clock news.

Trying

As we checked in at the front desk, the nurse handed us consent forms that contained various questions pertaining to the procedure. One asked us what we intended to do with any leftover eggs or embryos, in case Oliver and I divorced or one of us died. That's a scenario neither one of us had even considered. We checked the "We'll decide later" box.

They called my name as soon as we sat down in the waiting room. I jumped up, hugged Oliver, and headed for the big double doors. The nurse handed me a hairnet and booties.

"Do I really need these?" I asked, recalling the ones I'd worn for so many previous surgical procedures.

"What? You're worried about ruining your hair?" Dr. M. asked.

"Not at all. I'm just trying to keep positive, and these remind me of some not-so-great moments."

"Don't worry, Barbara," he said, helping me on with the hairnet. "We're going to take good care of you."

I lay down on the table and waited for a few minutes before they gave me a mild anesthetic. Before I could even finish praying to God that this would work, I was under.

I woke up when I heard Oliver and the doctor walking over to my bed.

"Everything looks good," the doctor said. I sat straight up so I could see Oliver's face while the doctor spoke to us. I was so relieved. He explained that they had retrieved seven good eggs and two medium-grade ones. Then, turning to Oliver, he said, "In a little while, the lab will take your sperm, surround each of the eggs, and leave them overnight to allow nature to take its course."

"I'm glad something about this process is natural," I joked. He didn't laugh. Nice guy, but I don't think he gets my humor.

Oliver's turn. By now, he had become very casual about having to produce in a cup. This time, though, he needed to perform right away and in a hospital. When Oliver was finished, he met me in the waiting room. I knew he would never say anything about it until we were outside, so I controlled myself.

"So what was it like?" I asked, while we were hailing a cab.

"It was nothing," he said. I looked at him disapprovingly. "After what I've been through, I expect a little more information."

"O.K." he continued. "A nurse led me into this room and handed me a cup. When I was done, I knocked on this little door and placed the cup behind the door."

"Was the nurse pretty?"

"I don't remember."

"Were there magazines in the room?"

"Yes."

"Did you look at them?"

"No."

"Well you had to have thought about *something*. Did

you think about the nurse who brought you into the room?"

"Barb, I thought about you."

"You did not."

"I did."

Look how much he loves her. Give them a baby.

Over the next three days, the doctors would monitor the fertilization process. As I imagined Oliver's sperm trying to find their way into my eggs, I kept picturing the clear plastic Petri dishes from my 9th grade science class housing the gonads of my frog, Seymour.

"Nobody leaves this room until I see names on your containers!" my teacher, Mr. Greenberg warned. "You don't want to come in here tomorrow and have to deal with someone else's frog's problems."

I was praying my problems were behind me. There was nothing more I could do to make fertilization happen—which, in a way, felt like a relief. It was somebody else's turn to do their job. It was my job, however, to prepare my body for implantation. Every morning, I had to insert a suppository containing progesterone, which preps the uterus to maintain a pregnancy. And in addition to the estrogen I'd been taking orally, I was given an estrogen patch as a booster. I also took antibiotics to prevent infection. I felt as if my body was some kind of space vessel that I was preparing for a voyage to an unknown planet.

The doctor called to tell us that Oliver's sperm fertilized four of my eggs and that the transfer would be in two days. Oliver planned to bring his cell phone to the hospital so he could call his father in California and let him know the minute the transfer was completed. We also decided to tell a few close friends and family so they, too, could say a prayer for us.

The night before the transfer, I realized that it had been two years since we first started trying on our honeymoon—not all that long, considering some of the stories I'd heard. But in that time, I felt a great distance had been traveled and, no matter what happened next, the journey had taught me a lot about myself.

Moondance

The day of the transfer, I was much calmer than I expected, just like I was on my wedding day. That day, my biggest fear had nothing to do with obsessing over whether or not my flowers would arrive on time or if the band would play the right songs or if the sun would shine for our outdoor wedding. My biggest worry was wondering how I would feel getting married without my mother and father beside me. Was I crazy giving myself a traditional wedding, when two of the most traditional elements of a wedding were missing? I had also chosen to walk myself down the aisle—not that my brother wouldn't have been honored or one of my parent's friends wouldn't have gladly stepped in. But my single years had been such a transition from loss to independence that I wanted, needed, to walk down the aisle alone—or at least halfway until Oliver would meet me. Miraculously enough, I was never overcome with the pain of loss that day. I missed my parents. I thought about them from the moment I woke up. I even tried to make myself feel sad or have a good cry before the girl came to do my make up, but sadness never came. I felt the same way today—ready for a new part of my life to begin and strengthened by all that had come before.

When Oliver and I entered the waiting room, we were greeted by two babies crawling around on the floor. One got lifted onto a lap by a man who looked like he was in his fifties. The other was being fed pretzels by a woman closer to my age. The two adults had apparently become fast friends. We couldn't help but hear that both of their babies were going to turn one the next week as they chatted about their families and their respective IVFs.

"My wife is inside transferring four," the man said. "They say four is a good number. I don't know why they say that, but four is a good number."

"We're getting four as well," the woman said. "We tried for three years and eventually adopted him. Now she's agreed to do this," she said, tilting her head toward the metal doors I was eager to go through. "She never liked getting needles and didn't want to go through all the injections. But then last spring, we came in and here we are." And just then, her partner came out and sat down.

"They told me I could wait out here until they're ready for me," she said.

It all seemed so casual.

When they called me in, I motioned to Oliver to come with me but the nurse stopped him. Unlike when I had inseminations, Oliver was not allowed into the operating room. The nurse led me to the dressing room and, after I changed into my gown, paper booties and cap, she offered me a Valium. I hesitated.

"Take a Valium," she said. "Why not? You deserve it." She was right, so I did. However, I didn't feel any more relaxed when I went into the surgical room. It was all very odd, me lying there listening to a Van Morrison CD while a woman doctor who reminded me of one of the doctors from *E.R.*—*the impersonal one*—picked up the syringe filled with the embryos of my future children. (My doctor doesn't handle the transfer. That's done by people specifically trained in embryo selection and implantation).

"What's your name?" she asked.

"Barbara," I answered, knowing she needed to be certain that I was the person whose embryos she was holding.

"Barbara what?" she continued, walking towards me.

"Barbara Nuddle," I answered. Hearing me recite my name only made the experience seem more surreal.

"I just want to make sure I'm giving you the right stuff," she said coolly.

"Thanks!" I said, laughing nervously. I wondered if she had any children and, if so, how she got them.

The nurse put her hands on top of mine. I loved that. It made me feel cared for. I listened to "It's a fabulous night for a . . ." and before Van got to the word "moondance," the doctor said, "That's it. They're in."

"You can lie here if you want to for a few minutes," the nurse told me as she prepared to wheel me into an adjacent room filled with other beds. "But after that, you can feel free to pee and leave."

That's it? There was no lying in bed for hours like I'd read about. No drifting in and out of slumber listening to Yani on my Walkman while sending good vibes to my uterus. After only 20 minutes of resting with my feet higher than my head, I got up, got dressed and left. Oliver and I went to our local diner for tuna melts.

Dr. M had suggested I avoid "any activity that you'll regret having done if this doesn't work." The entire weekend of my transfer, I never left the house. While I lay on my couch wondering whether Emeril's kitchen had a trash can on the other side of the counter top or if he was whisking the carrot tops right onto the floor, I tried to keep my mind off my uterus. I walked out to my hallway once to put the invites to Oliver's party down our mail chute. The rest of the day I kept my feet up. The hope was that the embryos take hold and your body begins producing more and more progesterone to maintain the pregnancy. I was scared, but I allowed myself to get my hopes up. When I called my friend Birgitta to tell her to light a candle for luck, I assured her I was also trying to prepare myself if it's a "no."

"Barb, she said, "you, of all people, are strong enough to handle the disappointment. Why not enjoy being excited and hopeful?" Amen.

The first week wasn't hell. The second one was. I went to my gym—a little. I walked on the treadmill—*slowly*. And I stared a lot at my belly thinking there was an almost-life inside me. Tick. Tick. Tick. I had never been this close before. To help pass the time, I watched a lot of old movies. Oliver had a new job producing celebrity profiles and his first assignment was Burt Reynolds. That meant he (we) needed to watch all of Burt's work, which, unfortunately included three *Smokey and the Bandits* and two *Cannonball Runs*. However, his work also included one of my favorite films, *Starting Over* starring Jill Clayburgh. I loved that Jill made herself candlelit dinners even though she was eating alone. I loved that she was so nervous on a date that she stuffed toilet tissue under her armpits. Jill C. was a role model of mine for years. I imagined her perpetually single and neurotic, even though I used to see her walking around the Upper West Side pushing a stroller.

During the second week, Oliver and I also managed to drive down to the Jersey shore to visit our friends for a few days. I spent a lot of time watching their one-year-old daughter walk around the room by holding onto the sofas and chairs. Her face alternated between determination and joy. I decided that if this cycle didn't work, I wasn't going to give up trying.

The morning of my pregnancy test, the nurse took blood from my arm and wished me luck. As the nurse was giving me a bandage, my doctor poked his head in the doorway.

"I know I'm not," I told him. "I feel absolutely nothing."

"You wouldn't feel anything," he assured me. "You're on way too many drugs to tell what's causing what. I'll call you around two o'clock with the results."

I looked at my watch. It was only 10. I had four hours to kill so I decided to walk down Madison Avenue to check out the stores. I stopped at a café and ordered a pot of chamomile tea and a slice of toast. That cost 12 dollars—pricey even for the East Side. But I indulged, promising myself that if I *was* pregnant, I'd bring my child back here someday to show him (or her) the table "where Mommy sat on the day she found out she was pregnant with you." I lifted the bandage from my arm and put it in my wallet—something else to save if it was a "yes."

I got home a little after one o'clock, turned on the television to the Food Network, and pretended nothing was more important than understanding the various uses for a daikon radish. Oliver came home from work at 1:30. He switched the channel to the news. When the phone rang at 2:43, I needed two rings to gain my composure before answering. Oliver was beside me, watching my face. I stared at the TV screen and focused on the word CNN as I gave Oliver the thumbs down signal while I heard my doctor say—for the second time—"I am so, so sorry."

"It's O.K.," I said, not wanting to make *him* feel any worse. He must hate making these calls.

"We'll know more next week," he said. "By then, we'll have looked at your lab results to learn what may have happened."

Oliver started asking me questions that I should relay to the doctor. Instead, I handed him the phone. It didn't work. That was all I needed to know. Besides, I needed to leave the living room because Pashko, our handyman, had been working in one of our closets and was calling my name. I'd begged Pashko to finish his plastering by late morning because I know how life is. I knew that he would show up at our apartment the exact moment we wanted to be alone.

"Barbara," Pashko called. "Come here and have a look!"

I went to the back room to look inside the closet that he had been plastering.

"Great," I said, with apparently too little enthusiasm.

"No, look *all* the way inside," he said. "I want you to see how smooth I made for you these walls."

"They look good," I said.

"Barbara, I can see by your face that you don't know much about plastering. But let me tell you, *this* is a beautiful job. A beau–ti–ful job. You won't have any trouble any more. I promise."

"Thank you, Pashko. You really think so?"

Home For The Holidays

Even though I never really felt the signs of pregnancy, I had never felt more like I was supporting a life inside me. My failed IVF cycle felt like what I imagined an early miscarriage might feel like. But in the eyes of some of our friends, it was merely a failed procedure and they treated me as if I had fallen off a bicycle.

"This was only your first one, right? Well, my neighbor went through four!"

After all the shots, the surgeries, the hope and, finally, those two long weeks of wondering if I'd get to go home for the Jewish holidays and tell my family I was pregnant, *it didn't work*. It was almost Rosh Hashanah—the Jewish New Year. I needed to call my brother to discuss which night we were eating and where during the High Holidays, and to give him the bad news.

My brother already told me that he'd be having a different "crew" for dinner this year. The only children present would be my niece and nephew. Remarkably—thankfully—I think he and Jill arranged it that way just in case Oliver and I wouldn't feel like being around a lot of kids.

"It didn't work," I said, the minute he picked up the phone.

"I'm *sorry*," he said.

"You know, all I wanted was to be able to come to your house for the holidays this year and tell you I was pregnant," I said, crying as I reached the end of my sentence. I couldn't remember the last time I was that open with my brother.

"I'm sorry," he said. "I don't know what else to say."

"It's O.K. You don't have to say anything," I told him, and meant it. Being able to share grief of any kind with my brother was helpful enough.

"By the way," I said, "I bought a Ralph Lauren coat the other day. It was a fortune so I shipped the box to your house to save on tax. I've been shopping like a crazy woman. Don't even open it up. I'm sending it back."

"You *should* buy yourself something," he said. "After

Trying

all you've been through, you should be very, very nice to yourself."

"I've been waiting 10 years for you to say that," I said.

Well, Billy. One time, Mommy had a special operation to make a baby but it didn't work. For the next few weeks, she was very sad. She didn't even think about making a baby. Then, sometime around Rosh Hashanah, in your Uncle David's guest bedroom, we planted the seed for you. And guess what?

The Latest Chapter

A Reunion

One night, Oliver and I were sitting with some friends at a café in Riverside Park. Suddenly, someone passed in front of our table, stopped, looked directly at me and said, "Bar–bie Nuddle!" That always means it's someone from my past because nobody in New York calls me "Barbie."

I looked at this woman, who looks exactly like she did standing next to me at the Comly School lost and found almost 30 years ago, and I said, "Deb–bie Albert." I couldn't believe it!

"Oliver! This is Debbie Albert, the girl from the lost

and found. The person who taught me the word 'Fuck!'" I screamed.

A few people looked over. I didn't care. This was Debbie Albert. I was amazed. What could this mean?

"This is my husband, Oliver," I said.

"Husband?" she asked. "Oh yeah, I forget people our age can be married."

I knew exactly what she meant. She, like me, had led a different life than many of my friends, particularly the ones from Philadelphia who married right out of college.

"Don't worry," I said, not wanting her to feel as if I thought she should be married, too. "It's only been a couple of years."

My mother was never thrilled with Debbie Albert. She never understood what we had in common. Debbie's parents had been divorced, her stepfather bought her a minibike when she was nine, and she was allowed to order her dinner in from restaurants I didn't even know delivered.

"You mean you just call up the deli and say you want a hamburger and they bring it over?" I asked, while sitting in her kitchen watching her unwrap the tin foil. "And your mother leaves you money for this?"

As she pulled up a chair to have a drink with Oliver and me, she said, "I'll bet you don't remember my old last name."

"Waldman," I answered.

"I can't believe you remember that!" she said.

"I do, and I remember that your mother brought in cupcakes to celebrate when you were officially adopted by your stepfather and changed your name to Albert."

"Wow," she said, not used to seeing someone who knew her when. "We can not let this go."

"No. We can't," I said, secretly hoping our chance reunion might signal something in my reproductive organs. We exchanged phone numbers and promised to have dinner soon, preferably before our twentieth high school reunion, which was two months away. Yet, seeing Debbie already felt like the best part of a reunion; remembering a part of myself, my history, my home. In spite of the disappointments, it seemed like my life was getting fuller.

It would take a few days before we would learn if another IVF was possible, and the thought of facing several more months of down time scared me. One day, I spent four hours traversing the city buying tubes of lipstick I didn't need in order to get Clinique's "free gift with purchase." Except for the travel-sized moisturizer I'd convinced Oliver *he* needed, nothing in the floral plastic purse interested me. I didn't care. I just needed to be part of someone's "Fall Bonus" excitement.

When I was in college, I worked behind the Clinique counter in Wanamaker's. I loved my little white coat and the faux silver "C" pin that was attached to my collar. I coveted all the free makeup they sent you for representing their company. And my mother looked forward to coming into Wanamaker's while I was working. She'd head for the sportswear department, located at the other end of the store behind accessories and fine jewelry, hold up a hanger with a sweater and matching skirt and yell, "What do you think?" When I would ignore her, she'd send over a salesperson to my counter.

"Are you Barbie?" the woman asked. Oy! She said "Barbie." This couldn't be good. "Yes?" I answered, still hoping she wanted an exfoliating demonstration.

"Well, your mother is in the dressing room and asked me to tell you she needs your opinion."

Working in cosmetics made me feel important, mature and professionally qualified to promote the merits of collagen night cream even though I was 19 and had never experienced a wrinkle. But now, as I approached 38, while debating between purchasing the all-day moisture gloss or the transparent lip stain, I'm trying not to think about the lost elasticity in my skin or the gray hairs appearing on my head. Will my child ever know me while my legs are still thin and my hair color my own?

When my mother was 38, I was eight and I remember her taking me by train into Center City for the first time, holding my hand and teaching me the names of the streets as we walked along. These past few weeks, I feel eight, again. I'm in the lunchroom, sick to my stomach, and I want to go home.

My friend, Mary, had her baby—a boy. Her husband called to tell us the good news. I had yet to call her with my congratulations because, for the first time in my life, I was afraid of the inevitable question, "When are you coming down to meet him?" I rehearsed the line, "I'll come when I can," before picking up the phone. How can you act uninterested to one of your oldest friends? Thankfully, Mary was the one who said lightly, "It's a zoo here so don't even worry about coming! Come when you can."

I hung up the phone and stared at my desk calendar. Another month of unmarked squares indicating when my next fertility treatment would begin. I reminded myself to appreciate all that I had. I called Jeptha. Whenever I'm on the phone with her, I can count on having a laugh. She and her daughter had moved back into her parents' home after a bitter divorce. Lately, Jeptha told me, she'd been avoiding shopping malls on Saturdays because the sight of happy families strolling merrily past made her sick. We soothed each other's wounds with rounds of "this was not how it was supposed to be." Jeptha left the garment center years ago because, more than anything else, she wanted a baby. I left the garment center because, more than anything, I wanted to find myself. At least we got that.

Barbara Nuddle

* * *

The other day, I went back to Barney's to exchange an overpriced Italian raincoat for the next smaller size. I'd never spent so much money on a coat but, after spending all this money on trying only to have nothing, Oliver insisted on buying it for me for my birthday.

"Trust me, it's great!" he said, just like one of my fashion friends would have said. "Besides, I love seeing you in it."

On my way to the store, I sat on the cross-town bus feeling guilty about keeping such a coat. I guess this is my life now, I thought. I've officially become one of those women who look sensational on the outside but are suffering on the inside. Just then, I noticed an older couple getting on with a child. The woman and man were Caucasian and their daughter was Asian. I assumed that, after years of trying, the couple chose to adopt. The little girl was singing, "Hi–ho, the derry–o, the farmer in the dell!" The woman noticed me watching them. I was simply wondering if I could do what they did—adopt a foreign child.

A year ago, after meeting several Asian babies in the park with names like Su Lee Goldberg, I announced to Oliver, "I don't think I could raise a Ming Nuddle." Now I know that I could. I have since realized that choosing to have a child should not be about raising a mini version of yourself. Besides, as my gynecologist told me, there are agencies that specialize in locating Eastern European children if that would make me feel more connected to my heritage.

Just then, the brakes on the bus screeched as it came to a sudden stop. I looked down at my hands, which were clutching my bag from Barney's. The mother was clutching the waist of her daughter as she kissed the top of her head. I couldn't help but wonder which one of us was getting on with their life.

S–E–X

Oliver's surprise party was in five weeks. It's always something—an anniversary, Valentines Day, Christmas, Hanukkah, the first day of spring—always a date by which I wanted to be pregnant. But by this time, I knew I couldn't become pregnant in time. As I finished the final preparations, I didn't want to think about infertility. I just wanted to cherish the days when I could forget we were trying.

Then one night, I was sitting on the couch with Oliver, grateful to be spending a relaxing evening devoted to Chinese food and "Must See TV."

"You know what tomorrow is?" Oliver asked, looking at me in a mysterious way.

"What?" My mind raced. Maybe he was surprising

me. We'd hoped to take a small vacation, but with the Jewish holidays and his work schedule, it didn't seem feasible. Maybe we were going away after all.

"Friday?" I said coyly, thinking it would be very like Oliver to book us for a weekend away at his favorite bed and breakfast in Vermont.

"Well, yes," he says. "It is Friday. But tomorrow is also your day three.

"Day three?" I gasped. "You're seriously thinking we should try and inseminate this month?" We'd talked about possibly doing it again before making a decision about another IVF. But now? Tomorrow? I had to go back in there tomorrow?

"I'm not ready to go in there yet," I told Oliver. "I don't want to hear about my FSH number. I can't stand to hear about that number for one more minute!"

I wanted to try. But I was scared of hearing what the doctors will say when we tell them we want to keep going. I didn't want them to think I couldn't face reality. I wanted to move forward and stand still at the same time.

"I'll tell you what," I said, feeling like a cow going to slaughter. "You call the doctor. If he says it's feasible, I'll go in to be tested. But, I do not want to hear anything about numbers. I swear to God. I do not want to hear—good or bad—what the number is. I just want to know whether or not we can go ahead with an insemination."

Oliver called. I went.

I sat in the waiting room copying a recipe for "Zingy

Trying

Lemon Squares" from *Women's Day* magazine. I always wanted to make lemon squares, and at this point in my life, I was grasping at anything that would make me feel productive. There was one other woman in the waiting room with me. When the exam door opened, a doctor I had never seen before came over to her and told her how happy he was that she produced so many good eggs. He wished her luck for her upcoming transfer. I'd never heard this kind of waiting room conversation and was particularly sensitive after my last cycle left me with no eggs to spare. I focused on my notepad—8 lemons, a cup of sugar, ½ cup of flour.

The door opened again and a baby boy came running into the waiting area, followed by his mother and father.

"He's great, isn't he?" his mother said to the woman about to have the transfer. "He's from here," she said, as if we were in Toys"R"Us and he was a stuffed animal. "We're back to try for our second."

I looked up and pretended to be deep in thought as I eavesdropped on their conversation. The egg woman smiled at the mother and said, "Are you going the whole route—IVF, I mean?"

"No," she says, brushing her child's hair with her fingers. "Just an insemination. And we got him on the first try."

OH MY GOD! These people actually exist? I forced myself to focus on my lemon square notes, then started ripping the entire recipe section out of the magazine.

Fuck it. I don't care if this is an office copy. This place owes me that much. I folded up the papers and put them in my pocketbook with a guilt-free gesture that suggested the article I tore out was about a treatment for cancer I must tell my dying friend about.

"Are *you* having an IVF?" the boy's mother asked the seated woman.

"Yes," she said.

"Are you nervous? Have you done it before?"

"I'm a little nervous, but I'm happy to be trying this method because I've had three miscarriages."

Well, O.K.! Now we're talking. She's had heartache. We can be friends. I gave her a sympathetic look.

My turn finally came, and when my doctor entered the examining room, he was very sympathetic about my failed IVF cycle.

"One of these days," he said, putting on his latex gloves, "I want to be able to give you some happy news."

"Me too," I said, holding back the tears. "I'm worried, though, that this won't be a good month for my FSH."

"Your husband told me I'm not supposed to talk to you about FSH," he said, guiding me up on the table. Oliver can be amazing.

Turns out my numbers were respectable, so this *was* a good month to try. I went back to injecting my thigh for a few days and waited for the nurse to call with further instructions. The day before the insemination, the nurse left a message at Oliver's office. Ever since my initial request, the office kept calling him, not me, with all my dosage information.

"Mr. Miede. This is Becky from Dr. M's office. Tomorrow is your insemination so tonight, at 11:00, give your wife her HCG shot. Also, we do not want you and your wife to have . . ." and, after pausing, she spelled out, "S–E–X." Then she continued, "Tomorrow, you are to 'produce,' bring it to the lab and have the insemination. Afterwards, at bedtime, you are to have S–E–X. I repeat, *after* the insemination, you are to have S–E–X."

Oliver played me the message. We were hysterical.

"Is this what she usually says to *you*?" he asked.

"Never!"

A week after the insemination, Oliver volunteered our services for *New York Cares*, a citywide community service organization. They put us on a bus going to Queens to be part of a clean-up crew for one of their elementary schools. Oliver and I were the oldest people on the bus but we tried not to let that bother us. Normally, sitting on a yellow school bus would trigger a flood of childhood memories for me. But, for once, I am in the here and now. I'm concentrating on my breasts, which feel like they are spilling out the sides of my bra. It's been over a week since the insemination and my bust is really big—bigger than ever, in fact. I'm also hot. I don't know if I'm feeling the glow of community service or early signs of pregnancy, but as Oliver and I begin cataloguing the school's library books according to the Dewey Decimal System, I'm sweating. I tried not to get too excited.

The night before, I hadn't slept well because the pain in my lower back was *that* intense. When I got home from our day of caring for New York, I called the doctor.

"When did we give you your HCG?" he asked.

"A week ago."

"O.K. That's good," he said. I think I detected excitement in his voice. "The first week it's the hormones that give you the symptoms. Now, this is your body talking. So, in this case, pain is good."

I'm excited but realistic. It's hard not to stay hopeful because I have never, ever felt like this.

The next day, Oliver and I took a road trip. We drove upstate to take a walk. "A *walk*," I kept reminding Oliver. "Not a hike." I wanted to keep my heart rate within the acceptable range. I reminded him of the weekend in Vermont when we first started trying. We took a steep hike up Mt. Abraham and I sweated through three layers of clothing before reaching the top. We joked that I was so overheated, I may have cooked my eggs. We laughed because, back then, even if it didn't work out, we knew we had lots of time. Or so we thought.

This time, after our walk along the river, I ate an entire turkey hero and a bag of cheese puffs. I was already treating my body to extras, as if I was pregnant. *This could be it.*

Oliver's party was one week away. The same day that my period—if I got it—was due.

"I think I am," I told my therapist. I *never* say that. But, it was four days after our nature walk and my chest was fuller than ever. "I just hope that, if I'm not pregnant, I get my period before Oliver's birthday party. Because if I get it on the day of his party, I'll be totally depressed that night."

I left her office and got my period that day.

Oliver!

The party was a success. For more than an hour, people performed songs from the musical *Oliver!* and made toasts in honor of Oliver's birthday. I chose to sing "I'd Do Anything." The fact that I can't carry a tune made it all the more special. I saw my friend Linda crying behind a plant. Later she told me how lucky Oliver and I were to have what we have with each other. She was right.

The day after the party, Oliver and I planned a trip—a big one. There is this *Roadrunner* cartoon where Wiley Coyote plants a box of Acme explosives into the ground. His plan, of course, backfires and it is he, not the Roadrunner, who explodes. He gets blasted so deep that his body drills through the earth and comes out the other side in China. I wanted that.

We decided we'd take a trip as far as our frequent flier miles would take us. Hong Kong, Japan, and Thailand were considered. The timing was good. The fertility labs would be closed for a couple of weeks in December. And thanks to a suggestion from Vince in accounting who suggested we pay for all my procedures with a credit card, we had accumulated enough miles to upgrade to business class! Oliver and I planned to leave after the Thanksgiving weekend, right after attending my 20th high school reunion. I had three weeks to go.

The Real Reunion

When I told my therapist I was going to my high school reunion, she warned me that most of the people there will be reaching into their bags or coat pockets for photos of their children. Sharon, my dental hygienist, told me, "The girls will look great. The guys won't." I'd gone to have my teeth cleaned so I could look dazzling to my former classmates.

"I thought it was the opposite," I told her. "That men aged better than women."

"No," she said. "The women are done having their kids and have gotten back into really good shape."

She's so sure of this. Why? Why didn't she consider women like me who had waited to have children?

As it turned out, she was right. Other than Debbie Albert and another girl from my class who was a lesbian (which certainly didn't mean she couldn't have children one day), I was the only person at my reunion who did not have children.

When asked to write their greatest accomplishment since high school for the reunion program, several women wrote, "Getting married and having my children." Not to take anything away from a joy I have yet to experience, but I always believed there ought to be more than that. Besides, I was living out a different story: the one about the girl who left her hometown to live in Manhattan and become famous at something she hadn't quite figured out yet. Then, when "the thing with her parents" happened, she thought she should do something brilliant like become a renowned authority on post-traumatic stress disorder. Or a photojournalist. Or move to Europe. I did none of those things. I lived. I searched. I felt reasonably good about my journey. That is, until the reunion. There, I had a hard time trying to define my life to a round table of women dressed in pastel suits who seemed oddly interested in me now, despite the fact that, in high school, they never let me stand by their locker.

I met a few women who, like me, had moved out of Philadelphia. These women also had children but wanted to talk more about missing the careers they left behind. They showed me their photos, acknowledged how cute their boys were, but knew there were other life choices. Perhaps that's why none of those women ever asked me why Oliver and I had no children.

The subject of infertility never even came up except with a guy who sat in front of me in my homeroom. In four years of high school, I'd never had a meaningful conversation with Anthony Moretti. Yet, somehow, on my way to the bar, he stopped me, wanting to catch up and tell me that he and his wife were going through IVF.

"Lupron, Progesterone, the whole bit," he said.

"I know, I know," I said, staring into a middle-aged face in search of the boy I once knew. "I just had a failed IVF cycle, myself. My husband and I are taking a trip and then we might try one more time."

Am I really standing at the Bucks County Sheraton, listening to strains of K. C. and the Sunshine Band while sharing infertility war stories with someone I barely noticed 20 years earlier? Bartender, another drink!

Thank You for Your Concern

While doing some pre-trip shopping in New York, I learned something new from the company that brings us Filofax. There, in between the "day-on-a-page" calendars and the "month-at-a-glance" inserts, I saw the latest addition in ways to organize our lives: the Filofax "Menstrual Diary." Filofax had printed a log of 28 days with a place for you to mark when your period began (P), when you ended it (E), and when you ovulated (O). Amazing, especially for an English company. I'd have thought they'd be a little more prudish about this sort of thing.

Trying

That's not all I learned that day. Apparently, Oliver and I had been trying to have a baby all wrong! We were supposed to be having sex every *other* day of the month, starting with day 10 of my cycle. Success guaranteed! Who said so? The girl in the shoe department at Saks, that's who. As she rang up a new pair of mules I wasn't exactly sure I needed, she gave me her theories on reproduction. Oliver, who had decided to splurge on new underwear, found me waiting patiently while the salesgirl took down my mailing address.

"Do you two have any kids," she asked, sizing us up as a couple.

"Working on it," I said, signing the charge card receipt and wondering if the shoes would be going back.

"You two need to do it doggy style!" she said, staring at Oliver and me.

"Uh-huh."

"Really!" she said. "Everyone thinks it's the other thing—the thing where you hold your legs up in the air. No! That's not it. Do it doggy style and, that way, your uterus is hanging down low when he comes inside of you."

She snapped off my receipt, which I promptly put inside my bag. I thanked her and started walking out of the store.

"I promise it works," she called out, wanting to convince me. "I told my girlfriend, Nicole, my friend Janine, and my best friend Trish the same thing and they *all* got pregnant!"

I guess this was my "gift with purchase." She wanted to help me make a child.

As Oliver and I walked home, the old pangs came back. It doesn't make any difference what we've been through in our efforts to make a child. I still get that same panicky feeling that leaves me wondering if we've been trying hard enough. I can't believe it! I thought I was past all this. But no matter how I'd tried to protect my soul as we bravely moved through our options and losses, I was still vulnerable.

The next night—and I was counting each one before Oliver and I left on our trip—I went to my friend, Irene's house for a small dinner party. There, I met several interesting women: a journalist, a poet, a musician and several photographers. A group of us started talking about teaching art to underprivileged children. Then the conversation moved to a book project the photographer was doing about a foster home. Coincidentally, the journalist told us about a story that she'd recently written about foster children.

"You know," said the journalist, "They say that parents who adopt don't make such great parents because of all they went through. Fertility-wise, I mean. It seems they place so much emphasis on the child becoming someone brilliant and accomplished that the child really suffers."

"Hmm," I said, sipping my wine. "Do *you* have any children?"

"No," she said, firming a grip on her wineglass. "I'm waiting. Do you?" she asked, checking out my credentials.

"No, but I've been trying."

"Oh!" the musician interjected. "My friends were trying and trying for their second child for *seven* years. They did everything—fertility drugs, IVF, everything. Then they just stopped. And you know what happened?"

Everybody join in!

"She got pregnant! So, the next time I see you, you'll probably be pregnant with twins," she said.

"Hope so," I said, finishing off my glass. Where is that bottle? I didn't want to give these women a fertility lesson that night. I didn't want to explain that it's not about relaxing or signing adoption papers or taking a vacation that gets you pregnant. What gets you pregnant when you're my age is that, one month, you have a good egg left over from God knows where since you're obviously past your prime, and your husband's sperm reaches that egg at the exact moment in your cycle when your egg is poised for action and you get pregnant. And even then, it's easier said than done.

I smiled. I didn't say to the journalist, "Don't wait. Run! Run as fast as you can to get your FSH tested so you know where you stand." These women were counting on me to be their next pregnancy-against-all-odds story. Maybe they needed to believe they still had time.

Far East

Our trip was everything we had wanted: adventure, beauty and a new appreciation for Japanese bento boxes (the fast food of Japan). Before we left, I worried that I wouldn't appreciate a trip to the Far East enough. I was never one of those people fascinated with the history of the Shoguns or had studied the art of Raku pottery from the Chiang Mai region. I was going to escape reality; to be surrounded by absolutely nothing that looked familiar.

When we arrived, I realized how much of the East has always been a part of my life—especially now. Had I not lain on a table while someone stuck needles all over my body in order to help me conceive? Didn't I brew teas from a Chinese apothecary, attend yoga classes in womb-harmonizing, and place crystals over my toilets to engage the proper feng shui? And let's not forget about all the sushi Oliver and I consumed on a weekly basis. My body belonged to the East. This trip would be a reunion for my soul.

Oliver and I loved being immersed in a totally different physical environment; a place where the trees, the birds, and the street signs looked foreign. Other than sushi, we had to order our food by pointing to photographs or plastic models conveniently located in restaurant windows. We also looked different to them. We were traveling at a time of year when there weren't many other American or European tourists. Oliver and I were clearly taller than everyone. It was easy for us to spot each other blocks away at a traffic light as we towered above the locals. Schoolgirls would giggle when we passed, or stop us to ask if they could take our photograph because they had never seen two people who looked like us.

We couldn't help noticing how cute the children were. Every morning in our hotel in Tokyo, we kept seeing the same three Asian children waiting by the elevator on our floor. We smiled and bowed to these adorable kids. Oliver and I wondered if God was trying to tell us something. I watched as two parents tried to teach their child to swim in the hotel pool. They looked older than us, which meant they started late, too. I couldn't help thinking. *It's not too late for us to travel with a family. Hang on.*

While in Kyoto, we witnessed Buddhist monks performing their meditations by raking intricate patterns in plots of sand surrounding their temple. Often the temple gardens were lined with trees and it was customary for passersby to write their wishes or prayers on a piece of paper and tie it to the tree. At one of the temples, we found a group of stones that were draped with what looked to be women's aprons. These stones, we learned, were gravestones for children lost through miscarriage.

I felt relief standing among these childlike monuments, comforted by the fact that this culture found a place for this kind of loss. At every temple, Oliver and I gonged the traditional bells, clapped, and made our offering. I wasn't praying for a baby as much as the strength to carry on.

Our favorite adventure was to a small village we had heard about an hour west of Tokyo that featured an onsen—a Japanese hot spring. We arrived by train, feeling slightly conspicuous as we wound our way through tiny streets in search of it. Unfortunately, the onsen we had in mind was closed for a local holiday—a fact we determined from the broken English of a receptionist at a neighboring ryokan (a traditional Japanese hotel). By using nothing less than pantomime, including scenes of us diving, swimming, and toweling ourselves off, we were able to communicate what we were looking for, compelling the receptionist to leave his post and lead us down the street to a waiting bus.

Despite the fact that we had absolutely no idea where the bus was headed, how long it would take us or how much it would cost, we got on. After years of trying to schedule and control our lives around conception, it felt great to just give it up and go with the flow. We quickly found seats in the back and smiled at the locals who seemed amused that two Americans ended up on their bus. It felt like the final scene in *The Graduate* when Dustin Hoffman and Katherine Ross ran from the church onto a city bus. After 10 minutes of climbing up a steep mountain road, the bus suddenly pulled over in front of what looked like a miniature temple and people started filing off. Oliver and I looked at each other and figured we had arrived. When we saw a photo in the building's lobby of a hot spring, we hugged each other in victory, only to be separated by a bowing woman who directed us to the male and female locker rooms.

Inside the onsen, the other women couldn't have been nicer to me as they pointed to my feet to let me know I should remove my shoes. After I took off all my clothes, they led me to a stall where they handed me a bucket, a ladle, and demonstrated how to soap and rinse myself before entering the waters. I could have lived without them standing there watching me, however. Once I entered the waters, there were other women seated along the side of the spring. They looked at me and smiled. "Beautiful," one said, nodding to the others, which made me think maybe they had never seen a nude white person before. One of the women said something to me while bringing her hand way up into the air that I *think* was the word for "tall." At this point, I decided to make myself look smaller by submerging myself into the soothing waters and floating towards a spot where I could see the nearby mountains. This was heaven. Suddenly, one of the women started splashing her hand in the water and I realized she was trying to get my attention. I watched as she left her spot and showed me where I could swim through a tunnel into another section where the waters were cooler. I did it and all the women smiled and clapped for me.

After about an hour of this, I was done. How much relaxing can a person take? I began to wonder how Oliver was doing. I tried to find a section of the springs that was within earshot of the men's section and started calling his name over and over. No response. It occurred to me that neither Oliver nor I had ever discussed how or when we'd meet once we were finished. Growing more and more frustrated and having no way to investigate myself, I sent someone into the men's section looking for a tall white man. Oliver rushed into the lobby dripping wet thinking I was in distress.

"Ready for lunch?" I asked, purposely ignoring the fact that I had just disrupted his zen experience. He laughed. We agreed to reconvene in a few minutes and then enjoyed a traditional lunch of soup, bento box and green tea in a tatami room overlooking the Japanese gardens while we compared notes of our experience. We were proud of ourselves for having found our way here. As beautiful as our day at the onsen was, our journey had been as exciting as the destination.

While in Thailand, Oliver and I visited magnificent gilded temples in Bangkok, hiked narrow mountain trails outside of Chiang Mai, and toured nearby food markets in search of exotic local delicacies. However, neither one of us considered roasted crickets a tasty bar snack. And then there were the elephants. Ever since working on the ranch, I never trusted animal rides at tourist attractions. Too many of the animals know they'd rather be somewhere else. It started out innocently enough. We were led to a clearing in the jungle bounded by a long wooden fence where we could safely observe and feed a herd of elephants as they were being bathed. Then we were invited to observe a demonstration of their logging skills, which is how these animals were originally utilized and valued.

"You know, we could go for a ride on these guys," Oliver told me as we watched one of the younger elephants carefully lift a log with its trunk and gently place it on a stack of others.

"Absolutely not," I told him. "I always get the feeling that, at any moment, one of these frustrated beasts is going to try to make a break for the border, and I don't want to be on its back when it does."

As we continued to watch Pantay and Tuk roll around in the dirt, we couldn't help but notice a young elephant charging up the hill with its driver—called a mahout—frantically trying to reign him in. I looked at Oliver and said, "That's exactly what I'm talking about. There's no way in hell I'm getting on one of these things."

As Oliver hoisted me onto the wooden chair that sat precariously atop our elephant, he assured me that we'd be safe, and we'd regret it if we missed this opportunity.

"Besides, I'm right next to you in case anything

happens," he added, laughing at my obvious nervousness. That turned out to be the worst part of a ride that went entirely too long. Every time Oliver shifted his weight, it felt like the whole chair was going to fall off, catapulting me into the jungle brush.

"Are you happy now?" I asked, as the elephant trudged on through the river. "Very," Oliver replied, hugging my waist.

Oliver and I loved living in our own travel bubble, undisturbed by anything that reminded us of life back home. That ended as we reached the beaches of Phuket, where we found ourselves among other American tourists. Our first day, I overheard a couple say they were from Philadelphia, but I refused to acknowledge them as they were the loudest people at the pool.

"O.K. Everybody. Who's up for crab?" a large man in floral swim trunks yelled, as he walked over to his group. "I made a reservation for eight."

I did not pick my head up. With my dark hair and Semitic features, maybe they'd think I was European. Odds are, they'd never hear me speak. Ever since we changed continents, Oliver begged me to keep my voice no louder than absolutely necessary. Loud Americans embarrassed him. Oliver often spoke in German just to disassociate himself from the occasional ugly countryman. Unfortunately, after five years of Spanish and countless years of Hebrew school, I still couldn't speak another language fluently and had to resort to speaking very softly. I don't think I opened my jaws to their normal capacity the entire trip.

On our last night, while enjoying our final Thai iced coffee, I heard a woman speaking particularly loudly from the table behind us.

"Herb, do you love this coffee? I swear to God I can get these exact beans at Ashbourne Market! It's called Thai Blend." I knew that the Ashbourne Market was an upscale food store in my hometown.

"Honey," the man apparently named Herb said. "I think you're thinking of Chai."

"Oh, Yeah, Maybe. But it's DEE-LICIOUS!!"

I turned to look at them, then back to Oliver. "That settles it. I said. If she's allowed to sound like that, I'm returning to my normal tone of voice."

Phuket also offered Oliver something he'd been craving for months—a beach. The warm air, lying in the hot sun for days on end where the only decision he needed to make was when to eat, sleep or read. That was his idea of relaxation. Not for me. I'm not a beach person. I hate sand.

Oliver, the California boy, has spent years trying to convince me of the merits of being near sand and water in order to relax. For me, the word beach always conjured up memories of my teenage years; going "down the shore" to Atlantic City where hundreds of people would bake on towels laid end-to-end. You couldn't even see the sand until a gust of wind came by showering beige granules that would stick to my well-oiled skin.

The one time I took a winter vacation at a beach was only because I had no money and one of my customers in the garment center offered to lend me her condominium in Puerto Rico. I tried to make peace with the sand on that trip. I found pleasure in swimming in the warm, crystal clear water, then returning to my chair and sipping a piña colada. I even went snorkeling. But seven days after I returned home, I had to get right back on a plane to return to Puerto Rico to recover the bodies of my parents.

For the last 12 years, the sight of palm trees surrounding a pool in the wintertime is an uneasy one. It reminds me of a time when I nervously sat on a lounge chair by a pool in Puerto Rico looking into those same leaves, waiting to hear if the authorities had any new information to report. There were days when the only thing I could do to keep from going crazy was to swim—often after sipping a Bloody Mary just to get my heart rate down. Back and forth, I went. With every stroke, I felt my heart pounding. It helped to listen to my breathing. Sometimes I'd hold it, then let it out with a yell just to let myself know I wasn't dreaming.

During those days, marked by the times the authorities would release the names of anyone whose remains had been identified, I remember looking toward the lounge chairs where my neighbor and his two daughters were being served a drink with a flower in it. They, too, were awaiting grave news. The regular hotel guests strolled around the poolside laughing, playing catch with a yellow beach ball and diving into the pool. A few pointed to us, then spoke in whispers. I'd jump back in the pool and continue swimming and breathing, swimming and breathing, testing my strength, reminding myself that I wasn't the one who died.

While sitting in my lounge chair by the infinity pool in Phuket, sipping a lemonade while waving to Oliver who was swimming laps, I noticed how the leaves from the surrounding palm trees were being reflected in the pool. Then I felt my stomach turn. It struck me, again, how a beautiful scene like this could be ruined by painful memories. It's the mother pushing a stroller. Or the happy family at the mall. Or the sight of daughters laughing over lunch with their mothers. All innocent images that ought to provoke smiles, not sadness.

Over the years, I've tried to fill my life with people, places and things that don't remind me of loss. But I've grown tired of diverting my gaze from things that are beautiful because I'm afraid they'll remind me of things bittersweet. You miss so much. I want to look.

Home

I can't believe I didn't see *this* one coming. No sooner

than we arrived home then friends of mine called and said, "So–o?"

"So what?" I asked.

"You two were gone for so long," they said. "And you *were* in Asia. We just figured . . ."

"What? You thought we'd be coming back with—a baby?" I only hoped they'd be as interested in hearing about our trip.

Actually, my views on adoption have changed over the past year, as did my ideas about what it means to be somebody's mother. If you want to bring a soul into this world, that's the job. And helping them become an individual is the most important gift I can give them. Not shaping them to look or be like me or Oliver. But this was not the time to go into all of that so I simply laughed and told our friends that, if necessary, that'll be our next trip.

Later, when I put all the photos of our trip in an album, I took pleasure in knowing that Oliver and I had had an amazing time together, even in the shadow of hoping for more.

Our dining room chairs arrived within days of our return. When these large "washable suede" chairs were placed around our dining room table, we sat across from each other and said, "This is it. We're really adults now." Most people say that when they become parents. We changed the rules.

Trying

After almost three years of trying, I have stopped trying to chart the astrological sign of my child-to-be. I'm no longer hoping for a boy or a girl. I don't even let myself think about baby names. What I have done is try to start seeing myself as someone who will eventually be somebody's mother. But it hasn't been as easy as that sounds.

This past Sunday, I lay on the sofa reading the Times searching the television guide for an old movie to *watch* that afternoon. I was happy to be hanging out with Oliver but couldn't help thinking about what most of our other friends were doing that day. Susan and Jay were bringing their son to a birthday party in the park. Linda and Ed were busy taking Kayla and Sarah to ballet class. Brad and Cimone would love to see us, but they had to drive Alex to his soccer match. Again, the feelings of emptiness and envy crept in.

Oliver and I decided to shop for a shelving unit for our living room to give ourselves a problem we could solve. The experience did not satisfy my nesting impulses as the process became overwhelming. One store gave us a series of pamphlets describing their "system" of shelving. If we were serious about finding the right unit for our needs, we were instructed to go home and map out exactly what our needs were. How many CDs would we expect it to hold? How many records? How many videocassettes? How many books? Are we interested in recessed lighting? Do we want to be able to expand the unit should our needs change? Wait a minute. Does everything we want in this world require such thorough examination of our desires and expectations? Can't we just walk in and buy something anymore?

When we came home, I sat down and sketched my vision of what a new wall unit would look like. I drew a space for my collection of art books and Oliver's vast LP collection from his DJ days. Then, just like I'd seen in a magazine, I created a lighted space on the bottom shelf where I envisioned large glass bowls or a contemporary vase. Oliver came over to see what I'd been drawing.

"Looks good," he said, "except for this part at the bottom. That's never going to work."

"What do you mean 'that's never going to work?' I saw it exactly like this in a magazine," I said, wishing he shared my vision.

"Barb," he said calmly, sensing my need to have something work out. "Having that opening on the bottom isn't safe."

I looked confused. He continued. "Because some day, we're going to have a child."

"Yes," I said, dragging the eraser across my sketch of the bottom shelf. Then I looked up at Oliver. "Yes we will."

Afterword

Barbara Nuddle was a writer, video biographer, and one of the most wickedly funny people I've ever known. She was also my wife and best friend. After surviving George Washington High School in Northeast Philadelphia, disco, and an older brother, she got a B.A. in Marketing at Temple University—a decision she often openly ridiculed as her interests clearly leaned toward the artistic. That was followed by ten years in the garment industry, where, she would say, she "learned to hang up clothes" and extol the "virtues of pink or teal." A shocking family tragedy led her to reconsider her choice of career and pursue a master's degree in Studio and Environment

Art at New York University and the International Center of Photography. Her works were displayed worldwide as part of the "Too Jewish?" exhibition, including the Jewish Museums in New York and San Francisco, the National Museum of American Jewish History in Philadelphia, and the Armand Hammer Museum of Art and Cultural Center in Los Angeles.

In 1997, Barbara began writing short stories about her life based on the years of journals she kept since she was in her early teens. Those stories, and subsequent ones she authored dealing with her struggle with infertility, led to the creation of this previously unpublished book. In May, 1999, the first chapter of *Trying* won her a grant from The New York Foundation for the Arts.

In the summer of 2010, Barbara was among the more than 22,000 women in the U.S. who are diagnosed with ovarian cancer each year. Despite promising early attempts to control the disease and the fierce determination and humor with which she faced all of life's challenges, she died in July, 2014. She was 53. As part of her legacy, I've decided the time is right to self-publish her work and let others enjoy her unflinchingly honest, irreverent and unforgettable voice.

During the writing of this book, Barbara insisted upon leaving her success or failure at conceiving a child an open question. She never wanted readers to think her path should be theirs. Since her passing, however, I've

Trying

come to believe she'd want readers to know that the last fourteen years of her life were among her happiest as she spent them being the proud and loving mother of our daughter, Sydney.

—Oliver

Acknowledgments

Thanks to Claire Merrill Kroll and Doug Richardson for their inspiration, editorial guidance and support. Thanks, too, to Karen Richardson for all her help with fulfilling Barbara's dream of getting this book published. And thanks to Barbara's many dear friends who encouraged her to keep writing and bring her stories to life.

www.ingramcontent.com/pod-product-compliance
Lightning Source LLC
Chambersburg PA
CBHW020317010526
44107CB00054B/1875